Images of War

The Story of the
Torpedo Bomber

Rare Photographs from Wartime Archives

Peter C. Smith

Images of War

The Story of the
Torpedo Bomber

Peter C. Smith

Pen & Sword
AVIATION

First published in Great Britain in 2007 by
Pen & Sword Aviation
An imprint of
Pen & Sword Books Ltd
47 Church Street
Barnsley
South Yorkshire
S70 2AS

ISBN 978 1 84415 607 8

Printed and bound in England
By CPI UK

Pen & Sword Books Ltd incorporates the Imprints of Pen & Sword Aviation, Pen &
Sword Maritime, Pen & Sword Military, Wharncliffe Local history, Pen & Sword Select, Pen
& Sword Military Classics and Leo Cooper.

For a complete list of Pen & Sword titles please contact
PEN & SWORD BOOKS LIMITED
47 Church Street, Barnsley, South Yorkshire, S70 2AS, England
E-mail: enquiries@pen-and-sword.co.uk
Website: www.pen-and-sword.co.uk

See all previous books by Peter C. Smith at the Author's Website:
www.dive-bombers.co.uk

The Gotha UWD Ursinus on her transport trolley outside the main Gotha factory at Gothe in 1916. *Franz Selinger*

The prototype Gotha WD-14, serial number 801. Later production models differed in tail and wingtip shapes and also in length and wingspan.
Franz Selinger

destroyer escorts were lured into leaving their secure anchorage at Moon Sound on 12 September 1916. At 5.45 p.m. the four German torpedo aircraft, led by a single engined floatplane with the squadron commander, took off from Angern See station. They were accompanied by ordinary bombers, which were to bomb the Russian warships and thus distract their attention while the torpedo bombers attacked at sea level. This was probably the first practical demonstration by an air force of the synchronised attack.

Twenty nautical miles north of Domesnes the *Slava* and five destroyers were sighted and were attacked by the bombers. The torpedo bombers turned on a parallel course to the warships to work their way into the best position to make a stern attack. At a distance of 1600 yards the torpedo bombers turned 90 degrees and released their missiles broadside to the battleship. By this time, one of the torpedo aircraft had dropped out of the attack owing to engine failure. The remaining three attacked at intervals of about four seconds. The first torpedo failed to run, because of damage caused by hitting part of the aircraft when released. The second ran short before diving to the bottom of the sea. The third ran straight and true, but one of the destroyers crossed the track before it reached the *Slava* and she was not sent to the bottom. Although anti-aircraft fire was intense, none of the

The Gotha WD-20 was developed from the WD-11 and the WD-14. *Franz Selinger*

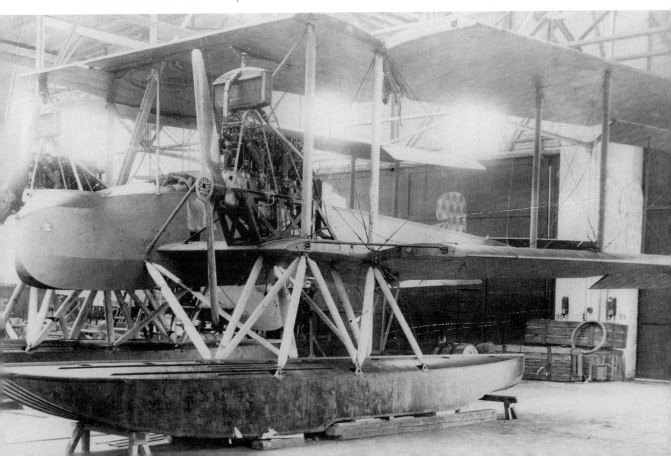

German aircraft was damaged.

The *Flugzeugbau* Friedrichshafen Company was another well-known producer of German single-engined seaplanes. It also, however, produced a twin-engined floatplane, the FF 41 A, nine of which entered service during World War I. With a span of 71 feet 6 inches and a length of 44 feet 6 inches, it was powered by two Benz 150-horsepower engines, giving a maximum speed of 78 mph and a range of 350 miles.

The second major type produced by Gotha was the WD 14. A total of seventy of this very successful aircraft was delivered to the Imperial German Navy. Generally similar to the WD 11, they were fitted with two Benz 200-horsepower engines driving tractor airscrews. The WD 11's span was 81 feet 3 inches and the length was 47 feet 1 inch with a maximum speed of 80 mph.

The final development of the Gotha series was the WD 22 a four-engined biplane with the engines in tandem driving tractor and pusher airscrews. The front engines were Mercedes D.III of 160 horsepower and the rear were Mercedes D.I 100-horsepower types. The speed was 81 mph and the range was 465 miles. Only two were built.

Austro-Hungary

One Gotha aircraft of the WD series, number 1661, was delivered to the Austro-Hungarian Navy Aviation on 4 July 1918 but was not used operationally. Also delivered was an improved Hansa Brandenburg GW known as the GWd. It was built as a single prototype with the number 701. It had a span of 79 feet, a length of 51 feet and was powered by two Benz engines of 220 horsepower each, which gave a speed of 80 mph. This aircraft was delivered to Germany's ally on 23 November 1917 after a ferry flight from Flensburg on the Baltic to Pola with various stops for fuelling.

Both these aircraft were to be fully tested in the Adriatic, but in the end were not used much as torpedo bombers. The Austro-Hungarian Navy was against the whole concept of the torpedo bomber because it was widely believed that the aerial torpedo would dive too steeply on entering the water and stick in the mud. This applied especially, it was thought, to the shallow waters of the Adriatic. Torpedo-bomber attacks were practical, it was assumed, only against moored ships.

Chapter Two:

The Inter-war Years

Although both Japan and the United States of America entered World War I on the Allied side, they were both too far from the European battlefields to exert much influence on aerial matters. But both had shown interest in the

A Japanese seaplane being hoisted out from its carrying vessel in the 1920s. Like its Royal Navy mentor, the Imperial Japanese Navy placed a high value on the aerial torpedo as a means of redressing the imbalance between the number of battleships in her fleet and that of her principal future opponent, the US Navy. Torpedo bomber attacks on an enemy fleet in its own bases had been a future option for the British, had World War One continued another year, and a surprise torpedo attack by destroyers on the Russian Fleet at Port Arthur had opened the Russo-Japanese conflict more than a decade earlier. A combination of the two methods thus naturally lent itself to Japanese thinking on any future naval conflict in the Pacific and was to come to full fruition in December 1941. *Author*

torpedo-bomber concept and, although they lacked war experience, both were to advance this concept more than other nations between the wars.

Japan

Japan set up the Naval Aeronautical Research Committee in June 1912, but little progress had been made by the end of the war. In 1922, two Blackburn Mk 2 Swifts were sent to Japan from Britain and based at Kasumigaura Naval Air Station forty miles to the north of Tokyo. Lieutenant Commander H.G. Brackley was sent to train Japanese pilots in torpedo-dropping and his success was to become only too evident fewer than twenty years later! The first Japanese carrier, the *Hosho*, was ready for trials at sea during this period. The Swift had a span of 48 feet 6 inches, a length of 36 feet and a height of 13 feet 3 inches. Fitted with a Packard engine, the maximum speed was 123 mph and the range was 300 miles.

The Mitsubishi B I M I Type 13 carrier-borne attack bomber was the next development in Japan, but in 1927 the Imperial Navy decided upon its replacement. In a competition, a Mitsubishi-sponsored Blackburn design, the Ka-3 two-seater biplane, was declared the winner. This was first flown on 28 December 1929 and was shipped to Japan from Britain early the following year. As the Type 89 a total of 205 B2Ms served aboard the carriers *Ryujo*, *Akagi* and *Kaga* between 1933 and 1937.

United States

In the United States, Admiral Bradley A. Fiske had proposed the adoption of the torpedo bomber type before 1914. Glenn Curtiss was the firm selected to build the first Navy aircraft, the A-1 Triad, which was first flown on 1 July 1911. In 1913, the base at Annapolis was set up and, on 1 July 1915, the office of Naval Aeronautics was established. Trials were carried out with torpedo bombers on 11 August 1917 but were failures.

After the Great War, Curtiss R-6Ls were modified to carry the naval torpedo. The aircraft was a two-seater with a 400-horsepower Liberty V12 engine. It had a span of 57 feet 1¼ inches, a length of 33 feet 6 inches and a height of 14 feet. The maximum speed was 100 mph and the range was 565 miles. Other types were developed in a determined effort to produce a torpedo bomber for the Navy in the 1920s and common features were in-line, water-cooled engines, biplane construction and interchangeable wheel or float chassis.

Between October 1922 and March 1923 three new American types and three Fokker Ft-1 twin-float monoplanes were tested at Anacostia. The aircraft selected from these tests was the Douglas DT-1. This was the first military aircraft produced by the Douglas Aircraft Corporation. With a span of 50 feet, a length of 37 feet 7¹/2 inches and a height of 15 feet 1 inch, the DT-1 had a range of 274 miles and a maximum speed of 99 mph at sea level. It could carry a 1835-pound torpedo.

Delivered in 1921, and exhaustively tested, the DT-1 was so successful that thirty-eight improved versions (the DT-2) were ordered and delivered in 1922 to the San Diego Naval Air Station, joining VT-2. By 1925 it had replaced the R.6L in Navy service. DT-2s were also used in test launchings from the first US Navy carrier, the *Langley* in 1925.

They in turn were to be replaced later by the Curtiss CS-1 of 1923, which was the first torpedo bomber, as such, produced by this company. Six joined VT-1 in April 1924. On 12 October 1925 the Martin T3M was contracted. With a steel tube fuselage this two-seater was powered by a 770-horsepower Packard engine and had a span of 56 feet and a length of 41 feet 4 inches. The maximum speed was 109 mph. In September 1926, they began to enter service with VT-1 aboard the *Lexington*.

Still dissatisfied, the Navy called for another torpedo bomber type and this resulted in the Douglas T2D. This two-seater biplane was powered by two Wright R-1750 engines developing 525 horsepower. The wingspan was 57 feet, the length 45 feet and the maximum speed was 124 mph at sea level. It could carry a 1618-pound torpedo for a range of 422 miles. The first T20-1 joined the *Langley* with VT-2 on 25 May 1927 and became the first two-engined aircraft to be launched from a carrier. The final American torpedo bomber of this period was the Martin BM, which was designed for the dual role of dive- and torpedo-bombing. Like most such compromises it could do only one job really well, and was used for dive-bombing until 1937.

Italy

As the originators of the torpedo bomber, the Italians had revitalised their earlier interest once the success of the British and German designs had become apparent during World War I. Both nations' designs had similar faults in that they were not powerful enough to lift heavy torpedoes without cutting down the weight of the warhead. Thus, in theory anyway, the weapon they delivered to the target was less effective than a standard bomb. Because of this the Royal Air Force and the *Luftwaffe* both concentrated on developing aircraft for conventional bombing throughout the 1930s. The Italians set about producing an aircraft capable of carrying a heavier torpedo. The Caproni Ca.44, which appeared in August 1917, formed the basis from which the later Ca.46 and Ca.47 were developed.

A mass crossing of the Atlantic by Italian Idrovolante S.55 torpedo bombers in 1933 brought home to the world at large, the potential threat to shipping from torpedo aircraft. *Ufficio Storico, Roma*

The Sopwith Cuckoo. *IWM Q67496*

Blackburn Dart. *IWM HU68294*

Great Britain

The Royal Naval Air Service had pressed on with successful designs and, by 1918, was far ahead of the rest of the world in performance and experience. Again, Sueter was the driving force and, in 1916, he got together with the Sopwith Aviation Company at Kingston-upon-Thames, already famed for its scout and fighter aircraft. The result was the famous T1, the Cuckoo.

The Blackburn Velos torpedo bomber was developed from the Blackburn Dart. *Royal Danish Navy*

Blackburn Ripon torpedo bomber. IWM Q92912

Blackburn Ripon. *IWM Q92900*

The Cuckoo was a single-seater biplane powered by a single 200-horsepower Sunbeam Arab engine, which gave it a speed of 103 mph at 2000 feet. The wingspan was 46 feet 9 inches, and the length was 28 feet 6 inches. It carried an Mk.IX 18-inch torpedo externally. The Cuckoo first entered service in July 1918, and ninety had been delivered by the time of the Armistice. Production continued post-war and Cuckoos went to sea aboard the *Eagle* in October 1918. The last were not finally phased out of service until 1923, by which time they had also served aboard the carrier *Argus*.

It was found that the 1086-pound torpedo was too light to inflict serious damage on ships and by the autumn of 1917 the Admiralty was seeking an aircraft capable of carrying the Mk.III 1423-pound torpedo, which had a 50 per cent larger warhead. Two aircraft, the Blackburd and the Sirl, were produced to meet this specification and after trials on the Humber in May 1918, the Blackburd was finally selected. The wingspan was 52 feet 5 inches, and the length 34 feet 10 inches. The single engine enabled the Blackburd to carry the heavier weapon at a speed of 90.5 mph. Meanwhile, the Blackburn Company had developed the T1 Swift as a private venture in 1919. The T1 Swift underwent trials at Gosport followed by deck trials aboard the *Argus* when Gerald Boyce piloted it. Successful results led to deliveries to the United States Japan, Spain and Brazil.

An improved version of the Swift was the T2 Dart. A single-seater powered by a 450-horsepower Napier Lion engine, it had a wingspan of 45 feet 6 inches, a length of 35 feet 6 inches and maximum speed of 110 mph at sea level. Following trials aboard *Argus* in 1921, the Dart was adopted as the standard torpedo bomber. Some 117 were built, serving at sea aboard the aircraft carriers *Argus* and *Furious*. The potential of the torpedo bomber was emphasised when, during combined fleet exercises off the Isle of Wight on 9 September 1930, an attack by fifteen Darts from Lee-on-Solent scored eight hits on Britain's latest battleships, the *Nelson* and *Rodney*.

The R.N.A.S. had become part of the RAF in 1918 and the RAF operated all aircraft from the fleet's carriers. In consequence, the development of naval aircraft underwent a dramatic decline. It was regarded as a backwater by RAF pilots and was voted very limited funds. As a result, during the late 1920s and the 1930s the Royal Navy's once commanding lead in the field of naval aviation was thrown away.

The Blackburn Velos was developed from the Dart and was a two-seater. The Velos was powered by a 450-horsepower Napier Lion V engine and was developed as a floatplane. A batch of sixteen was sold to the Greek Navy for coastal defence requirements after being tested by Guidoni himself and others in October 1925.

Blackburn's successful association with torpedo bombers continued in the late 1920s through the ugly Blackburn Blackburn to the elegant Ripon, which was the Dart's replacement in naval service. The Blackburn Ripon was a two-seater biplane, powered by a 750-horsepower Napier Lion XIA engine. The wingspan was 44 feet 10 inches and the length was 36 feet 9 inches. With a maximum speed of 126 mph at sea level and twice the range of the Dart, the Ripon was a very popular aircraft and first entered service in August 1929. Only ninety-two were built between 1928 and December 1933, which gives some idea of the lack of effort devoted to the Fleet Air Arm.

Another torpedo bomber with a Blackburn pedigree was the Baffin, which was

Blackburn Baffin torpedo bomber. *IWM MH27*

first flown by Flight Lieutenant A.M. Blake in June 1933. It was a two-seater biplane, powered by a single Bristol Pegasus 565-horsepower engine, giving a speed of 136 mph.

At the outbreak of World War II, the Royal Navy's front-line torpedo bomber was the biplane Fairey Swordfish. Ending Blackburn's long run of torpedo bombers for a short period, the Swordfish replaced the Blackburn Shark when it entered squadron service in 1938. The Swordfish was obsolete before the war began. Due to the dedication and fearlessness of the young Fleet Air Arm crews, the old 'Stringbag', as she became known, remained in service and covered itself in glory, but how much more could have been achieved with modern aircraft?

The three-seater Swordfish was powered by a 690-horsepower Bristol Pegasus II engine. The wingspan was 45 feet 6 inches, the length was 36 feet 4 inches and the maximum speed was 139 mph at 4750 feet. Later versions were powered by a 750-horsepower Pegasus XXX engine. First flown on 17 April 1934, the Swordfish was still serving operationally more than ten years later and its exploits were legendary. At the outbreak of the war Swordfish were embarked in the carriers *Ark*

A Fairey Swordfish landing aboard a British carrier. *Malizia*

Royal, *Courageous*, *Eagle*, *Hermes*, *Glorious* and *Furious*.

The RAF was even less interested in torpedo-bombing, and even as late as 1941 the front-line defence of Singapore rested on a squadron of obsolete Vildebeest biplanes with a top speed of less than 100 mph; by contrast their Japanese opposite numbers were employing sleek, state-of-the-art long-range monoplanes to carry the torpedo into action. The resulting debacle was predictable. One RAF officer appointed to command Coastal Command, where torpedo bombers ought to have been the front-line aircraft, confessed that he could not see any point in carrying a torpedo on an aircraft into battle at 250 mph then dropping it so it could proceed to the target at 50 mph. His mind could not grasp that a hole below the waterline was more likely to sink a ship (even a battleship) more readily than a bomb trying to penetrate many inches of armour decks, even in the unlikely event that the RAF could actually hit a moving ship, which proved almost impossible for them when it came to the test of war as they disdained dive-bombing as much as they did torpedo-bombing.

While Great Britain was diligently plodding on with biplane after biplane, gaining 10 mph or so with each new design, other nations were taking larger strides. The seaplane concept, however, died hard, even in Italy. A massed crossing of the Atlantic by Idrovolante S.55s in 1933 was given great publicity and the menace to ships from aerial torpedoes carried at such ranges was obvious.

Germany

When Germany began to rearm in the 1930s it might have been expected that, after the successes of World War I, the development of the torpedo bomber would have been given some priority. But Goering, like his counterparts in the RAF, was not interested in maritime affairs. As a result development rested solely upon the Navy and with limited funds it lagged. Again, seaplanes were the most favoured types. Even when the first carrier, the *Graf Zeppelin*, was laid down, her main offensive aircraft were to be Stuka dive-bombers.

The French tried the floatplane torpedo bomber approach in the 1930s, as they only possessed one aircraft carrier. This is the Latecoee Late 298 at anchor. *French Navy Official via Pierre Hervieux*

Chapter Three:

The Early War Years

Italy

The Italian air force, the *Regia Aeronautica*, experimented with radical approaches. The original role of the Savoia Marchetti SM.79-1 was as an altitude bomber in the Spanish Civil War. After repeated attempts at mass bombing attacks against the British Mediterranean Fleet in July and August 1940, it quickly became evident that altitude bombing against warships with the bombs and instruments of the day was useless.

The result was the conversion to the torpedo-bombing role of the SM.79-11, powered by three 1000-horsepower Piaggio P.XI engines, although the idea had been fostered for many years prior to the war. The SM-79 was to be one of the most outstanding of the land-based torpedo types and its name, the Sparrow, became as famous in Italy as the Spitfire was in Britain. Trials were held at Gorizia in 1937 with the standard 17.7-inch naval torpedo, fitted with a 375-pound warhead. Using a special rack offset from the centre line of the plane and a newly developed launching sight, this torpedo quickly proved itself. Attempts made later to fit the SM.79 with two such mountings were ultimately successful although they affected the aircraft's performance. The Italians established a torpedo bomber training school at Grosseto on Italy's west coast and, after many early conventional bombing attacks had failed against British warships, more and more squadrons were switched over to this type of warfare.

A tri-motor Savoia Marchetti SM 79 in standard Regio Aeronautica markings. It was originally designed for high-altitude level pattern bombing but this method failed to strike any British warships so the aircraft was modified as a torpedo bomber – with immediate success. *Ufficio Storico, Roma*

The Fiat BR.20-*Bis* was another standard medium bomber that underwent a similar adaptation to enable it to play a more prominent part in the air-sea war, which was so dominant in the Mediterranean theatre.

The Italians had devoted considerable resources towards the maritime aspect of their air force, no doubt with the view that any war with Britain and France would be decided ultimately at sea due to Italy's exposed position in the Mediterranean.

The SM.84 was adapted to carry a special device for use against warships and convoys known as the *Motobomba*. Colonel Lionello Leone who commanded 132 *Stormo* based at Bari described to the author the function of these weapons, which were in effect circling mines or torpedoes. Each SM.84 could carry two of these weapons, which had a weight of 400 kg. Leone described them as *naval* weapons, which were dropped perpendicularly by parachute. On impact with the sea the parachute automatically released itself. A gyroscopically controlled motor then started and at three-metres' depth a siphon of mercury started the motor and fins, which would drive the *Motobomba* forward with a spinning motion, without leaving any telltale wake behind it. They were self-destructive and had a maximum time allowance of twelve hours.

The Italian *Aerosilurante* units, although merely a small fraction of the total Italian air effort, made their mark on the air-sea battles taking place in the Mediterranean. Among this handful of pilots, several soon became famous for their skill and accuracy. They included pilots such as Deodato, Erasi, Mauri, Robone, Sabatini and, the most famous Italian torpedo bomber ace of them all, Carlo Emmanuel Buscaglia.

An early attack on Alexandria harbour on 15 August 1940 failed to materialise; however, the SM.79s were very active in daring twilight attacks at dusk and dawn on ships of the Mediterranean Fleet. No fewer than three cruisers fell to their torpedo attacks in the eastern Mediterranean during a two-month period. On the night of 17 September, a British naval squadron was caught returning from a bombardment of Bardia and an attack in brilliant moonlight by the SM.79s resulted in a hit on the heavy cruiser *Kent*. This was a particularly valuable result for the Italians because the *Kent*, which had 8-inch guns, had only recently joined Admiral Cunningham's fleet. Until the arrival of the *Kent*, together with the *York*, the British cruisers had been outgunned by the Italian ships. By torpedoing the *Kent*, the Italians partially maintained their advantage.

This initial success was repeated when the *Aerosilurante* made another attack on the fleet as it was returning to Alexandria after a sortie on 14 October. The fleet was attacked again at dusk and one SM.79 hit the light cruiser *Liverpool* in the bows. The explosion ignited a petrol tank, which in turn detonated her forward magazine. The whole of the *Liverpool*'s bows before the bridge were wrecked and hung down into the water. Taken in tow by the light cruiser *Orion* and destroyers, the crippled cruiser struggled back to Alexandria, the damaged bow dropping off on the way in.

Yet a third success took place on 3 December 1940, when the light cruiser *Glasgow*, newly arrived to replace the *Liverpool*, was caught by two SM.79s while at anchor in Suda Bay, Crete. The British warship was taken completely by surprise and no fire was opened against the Italians. Consequently, both aircraft were able to place their torpedoes firmly into the *Glasgow* at 3000 yards' range. Very severely damaged, the *Glasgow* was the third cruiser to limp back through the Suez Canal on a forlorn journey to the repair yards of Britain or America.

All these attacks were the work of one squadron, Buscaglia's 278 *Squadriglia*, operating in two sections based respectively at El Adem in Libya and at Rhodes in the Aegean. On 27 December, a second unit, 279 *Squadriglia*, finished its training at Gorizia and moved to the operational base in Sicily for operations against British convoys attempting to force the straits and relieve Malta. These two were joined by yet a third, 281 *Squadriglia*, based on Rhodes, in March 1941.

France

The French Navy's air arm, the *Aéronavale*, was not prominent at any time in the field of torpedo-bombing, and only a single carrier was operational pre-war. Due to this restriction they tended to develop the old concept of the floatplane, as indeed had Britain to a small extent and Germany almost exclusively. The rapid defeat of France resulted in no activity in their limited torpedo bomber force against the Axis. Two of France's most modern torpedo bombers in service prior to June 1940 were the Latecoere Late 290 and the Latecoere Late 298/01.

Germany

In Germany limited progress had been made during World War I with floatplanes. The German Navy, the *Kriegsmarine*, had a few torpedo bombers on its strength, the He.115 replacing the He.59 in the torpedo bomber and general-purpose role in 1938. This twin-engined plane was an advanced design for its time and its excellent handling qualities ensured that it remained in front-line service throughout the war. The Arado Ar.95, a single-engined floatplane powered by an 880-horsepower BMW-132-DC engine was designed for use as a catapult aircraft for German heavy ships. It could also carry the standard torpedo when required. Blohm and Voss was famed for its long-range scouting aircraft during World War II and the twin-engined BV-140 torpedo aircraft was another of its wartime products.

The main striking force of the German Navy's torpedo bombers was the He.115s. Good though these aircraft were, only a few were actually ready for operations on 3 September 1939, one *Staffel* only (nine aircraft) serving with the *Seeflieger* (Coastal) forces. They were used for minelaying as much as for torpedo operations.

This chronic shortage of torpedo aircraft can be laid partly at the door of *Reichsmarschall* Hermann Goering who had no understanding and little interest in maritime warfare. But an equally important factor was that between 1933 and 1940 the German Navy failed to recreate the success of its World War I aircraft and operations. In 1933, the Navy purchased the Horten naval torpedo patents from Norway as a first step and this was followed in 1938 by obtaining similar patents from Italy for the Whitehead-Fiume torpedo. Despite this, subsequent development was leisurely. During extensive torpedo-dropping trials, carried out in 1939, both the He.59 and the He.115 were used and the failure rate of the torpedoes was a staggering 49 per cent. This was due to aerodynamic difficulties in launching from aircraft, depth control problems and fusing failures.

So it was that the limited He.115 force operated by the Navy did not have a high success rate during the opening years of World War II. Only two dozen floatplanes were engaged in limited torpedo attacks on British convoys off the coast of Scotland and in the Western Approaches. The *Luftwaffe* ignored the torpedo bomber, carrying out its attacks with Junkers Ju.87 dive-bombers in coastal waters. These had great success in the Channel in the summer of 1940 and many victories in the

An Arado Ar.95 W, fitted with the 880 hp BMW DC engine. It was a general-purpose seaplane carrying a torpedo. *Franz Selinger*

A Blohm und Voss BV.140 prototype, still carrying her civilian registration. *Franz Selinger*

A Heinkel He. 115 B-1, being fitted with a trial torpedo at Potenitzer Wick for experiments. *Franz Selinger*

Mediterranean during 1941/2. Medium bombers were also used from time to time.

Few sinkings were therefore recorded by German aerial torpedoes during this period, and the scarcity of aircraft was worsened by an equal shortage of torpedoes. One lone victory was obtained on 23 August 1940 when convoy OA.203 was attacked in the Moray Firth and two ships were sunk and another damaged.

Japan

In Japan, the torpedo bomber developed in leaps and bounds, both as a carrier-borne and as a land-based aircraft. In 1932 the 7-*Shi* plan initiated a whole new series of all types. The results of this were disappointing but the 8-*Shi* plan of 1934 brought much better results.

The first step was the Yokosuka B4Y (Allied codename *Jean*), which was a single-engined three-seater carrier-borne biplane. The wingspan was 49 feet 2½ inches, length 33 feet 3½ inches and the height was 14 feet 3½ inches. The *Jean* could carry a 1764-pound torpedo into action at 173 mph and had a range of 978 miles.

A formation of Navy Type 1 Land-based Torpedo Bombers (G3K2), given the Allied code name Nell. These attack bombers could act as both conventional precision altitude bombers or torpedo bombers with the same highly trained naval aircrews. *Tadashi Nozawa*

A Japanese Navy aircrew pose with their Navy Type 1 Land-based Torpedo Bomber (G3K2), Allied code name Nell, on a Pacific base. The range and accuracy of such Navy aircraft came as a nasty shock to the British in 1941. *Tadashi Nozawa*

Three Imperial Japanese Navy Type 1 Nelly. This type was involved in the sinking of the British capital ships *Prince of Wales* and *Repulse* off Malaya in December 1941. *Tadashi Nozawa*

Japanese Navy Type 1 Land-based Torpedo Bombers (G4M2), given the Allied code name Betty. *Tadashi Nozawa*

When Japan ultimately entered the war in December 1941, this aircraft was widely believed to be the standard equipment of the Japanese Navy.

Also produced under the 8-*Shi* plan of 1934 was the Mitsubishi G3M2 (Allied codename *Nell*). This was a great advance in torpedo bomber design. Designated the Type 96 attack bomber, it was originated by Admiral Yamamoto while he was serving as chief of the Technical Division of the Naval Bureau of Aeronautics. This twin-engined sleek monoplane had a five-man crew and could carry a 1764-pound torpedo into attacks at a speed of 258 mph. It was land-based and had the outstanding range of 2,365 nautical miles. The wingspan was 82 feet, length 54 feet and height 12 feet 11 inches.

In 1940 the most advanced carrier-borne torpedo bomber in the world was the Imperial Japanese Navy's Nakajima BSN2 Type-97 attack plane (codenamed *Kate* by Allied forces). Produced under the 10-*Shi* programme of 1936, it first went into production in November 1937 (Model 11). By December 1939, the Type-12, a much-improved version, was entering service. A single-engined, three-seater monoplane, it was the first plane thrown into action at Pearl Harbor. Carrying the standard torpedo, the *Kate* had a top speed of 235 mph at 11,800 feet and a maximum range of 1,075 nautical miles. The wingspan was 50 feet 11 inches, length 33 feet 9^1/$_2$ inches and height 12 feet 2 inches.

The Mitsubishi G4M2 Navy Type-1 Land attack plane (codenamed *Betty*) was another land-based torpedo bomber of the Imperial Japanese Navy. Development of this aircraft began in September 1937, under a replacement programme for the *Nell*. Its outstanding feature was its range of 3,256 nautical miles. In addition, it was the first torpedo bomber to carry its torpedo internally. It had a crew of seven and a top speed of 272 mph at 15,000 feet. Its chief drawback was its lack of resistance to tracer and it earned itself the unenviable nickname the 'Flying Lighter' in battles over the Solomons in 1942/3. The wingspan was 82 feet, length 65 feet 8 inches and height 19 feet 8^1/$_2$ inches.

Air-to-air photograph of a formation of Japanese Navy Type 1 Land-based Torpedo Bombers (G4M2). *Tadashi Nozawa*

The US Navy's Douglas Devastator torpedo bomber. IWM A9377

United States

In the years leading up to World War II the US Navy had developed its own torpedo bombers. However, the Army Air Force had no interest in the torpedo, and therefore land-based long-range torpedo aircraft were not a feature of America's developments as they were in Japan. The Navy had pushed ahead with the design of carrier-borne aircraft. With the introduction of the new carrier *Ranger* in 1934, and with more carriers on the stocks, a new range of aircraft was being called for.

Prototype torpedo bombers were ordered from the Great Lakes Company and Douglas in June 1934, and from subsequent tests the Douglas TBD-1 was selected. It was the first US Navy carrier-borne monoplane to be put into production. Other features were upward folding wings, which were power operated, and a semi-

A Douglas TBM Devastator aboard the carrier USS *Yorktown* after an accident in September 1940. This aircraft was repaired and, as part of VT-8, was destroyed during the Battle of Midway in June 1942. *Naval Historical Center, Washington*

retractable undercarriage. Named the Devastator, it was a three-seater aircraft powered by a single 900-horsepower Pratt & Whitney engine. The torpedo was carried externally and at a slight forward tilting angle, which made this aircraft unmistakable in flight. The wingspan was 50 feet, length 35 feet and height 15 feet 1 inch. The maximum speed was 206 mph at 8000 feet. Orders were placed for 130 in 1936 and the first aircraft was delivered to VT3 on 5 October 1937. Devastators later joined VTs 2, 5 and 8. The Devastator was still in service at the start of the Pacific war and saw action at the raids on the occupied Marshall and Gilbert Islands and the attack at Lae, as well as during the first great carrier battles.

Devastators of VT-5 on the aft flight deck of USS *Yorktown* at NAS North Island in May 1940. Greater use of the flight deck by the USN enabled their carriers to accommodate more than twice the number of aircraft than the Royal Navy. *Naval Historical Center, Washington*

Great Britain

Monoplanes formed the backbone of the torpedo-bomber forces of the United States, Japan, Italy and Germany but the Royal Navy's front line equivalent in 1940 was a biplane. This was the Fairey Albacore, originally designed in 1936 as a replacement for the Swordfish. It featured an enclosed cockpit for the crew, an all-metal fuselage, hydraulic flaps and a remarkably economical engine. Despite these features however, its other specifications were years behind those of its foreign counterparts.

A Fairey Albacore with a torpedo mounted. Generally the aircraft was little improved on its predecessors since 1918 and it was replaced as quickly as possible after 1943. *Real Photos*

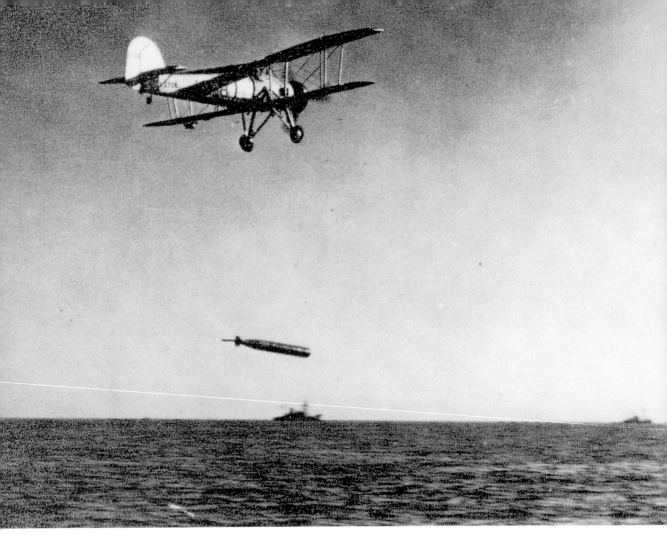

A Swordfish TSR drops a torpedo against a practice target. The need to descend to low-level and fly straight and true into the face of heavy anti-aircraft fire, surface fire or enemy fighters proved to be the torpedo bomber's nemesis as losses were inevitably high. When deployed against the German battle cruisers *Scharnhorst* and *Gneisenau* in the 'Channel Dash' in daylight, the failure of British fighter cover saw the loss of an entire Swordfish squadron. *IWM*

The Albacore was a single-engined, three-seater biplane. It was powered by a 1065-horsepower Bristol Taurus II engine giving a maximum speed of 161 mph at 4000 feet. The externally mounted 1610-pound torpedo could be carried a maximum range of 930 miles. The wingspan was 50 feet, length 39 feet 9½ inches and the height was 15 feet 3 inches. In May 1937, one hundred were ordered under an Air Ministry contract. The Fleet Air Arm did not finally revert to full Navy control until later. The result of twenty years of this arrangement was the low quality of the British torpedo bombers.

The first Albacores to go to sea joined the *Formidable* with No. 826 and No. 829

Squadrons in November 1940. They were soon in action and in March 1941 scored a hit on the Italian battleship *Vittorio Veneto* while the Swordfish of No. 815 Squadron hit the heavy cruiser *Pola*. This action led to the Battle of Cape Matapan and a decisive defeat for the Italian Navy at the hands of Admiral Cunningham's battleships. During the preceding air-sea battles, SM.79s tried to torpedo the *Formidable* but failed. The Albacores, led by Lieutenant Commander W.G.H. Saunt DSC, penetrated a heavy barrage to score their hits, which left the battleship limping home at reduced speed. The Swordfish left the cruiser disabled and she and two sister ships were later sunk by gunfire.

In March 1942, Albacores from *Victorious* made an attack on the German battleship *Tirpitz* when she sortied out against a Russian convoy off Norway. They failed to hit her, although several torpedoes ran close. Although employed on many fleet and escort carriers from 1941 to 1943, these were the only major attacks carried out by Albacores in the torpedo bomber role. In April 1942, Albacores came close to a duel with a Japanese task force in the Indian Ocean. Admiral Somerville planned to use them in a dusk strike against six big carriers, but in view of the reputation of the Japanese fighters it is perhaps fortunate for the Royal Navy that this one battle was not fought.

It is an ironical fact that the old 'Stringbag', which the Albacore was meant to replace, outlasted her in service and affection. It was the Swordfish that made the outstanding contributions to the Royal Navy's great victories in 1940/41. During the Norwegian campaign in April and May 1940, the Swordfish aircraft had their first chance to show their mettle. On the Italian declaration of war in June, No. 830 Squadron was established on the island of Malta. When the French fleet followed the orders of the puppet Vichy government, it was a Swordfish from the *Ark Royal* that carried out the first torpedo bomber attacks on battleships when it torpedoed the battle-cruiser *Dunkerque* at Oran on 6 July 1940. Swordfish aircraft also made the first attack on a capital ship at sea in World War II when they tried to stop the battle-cruiser *Strasbourg* escaping to France on the same occasion. Swordfish from the *Eagle* with Admiral Cunningham's fleet off Calabria struck at the Italian fleet on 9 July, but failed to score any hits.

Swordfish, operating from desert airstrips in support of the Army, scored the first of their many successes against the Italians, when on 22 August three Swordfish of No. 813 Squadron led by Captain Patch DSO, DSC, RM claimed a submarine, a depot ship and two destroyers in an attack on Bomba harbour in Libya.

Meanwhile, the RAF had introduced the Bristol Beaufort as a replacement for the Vildebeest torpedo bomber. Although the Beaufort was intended mainly as a torpedo aircraft of a faster type than hitherto available, early attacks made by these aircraft were made using bombs. The reasons for this state of affairs were that in early 1940 their crews were not fully trained in the new methods of torpedo-dropping and, like the Germans, the RAF had a shortage of torpedoes. In fact, when war broke out only two squadrons were equipped for torpedo-bombing in the RAF, these were No. 22 and No. 42 Squadrons and both were equipped with the Vildebeest. Beauforts replaced these in the spring of 1940. The Beaufort was a four-seater monoplane powered by two Taurus engines, which gave it a top speed of 290 mph.

The switch from the obsolete types to this much more powerful aircraft required new techniques and at Thorny Island and Gosport, Portsmouth, these new tactics were given their first tests. Because the Beaufort built up speed very quickly in a dive the old method of diving onto the target from beyond effective anti-aircraft range could not be used. Instead, the aircraft had to be at low level throughout the whole approach and it was thus exposed to prolonged fire from its target. Experiments with fitting dive brakes and trials with a new 'flying' torpedo, which could be dropped from 1500 feet, were not a success. This later device, known as the *Toraplane* was later to be developed by the *Luftwaffe*.

On completion of their training, the men of No. 22 Squadron moved to North Coates airfield in Lincolnshire under the command of Wing Commander F.J. St.G. Braithwaite. They carried out their first torpedo-bombing mission on 11 September 1940, when five Beauforts led by Flight Lieutenant Dick Beaumont struck a convoy between Calais and Ostend. Three torpedoes 'hung up', one exploded prematurely but the final one ran true and destroyed a large merchant ship. All the Beauforts returned safely to base.

Because of the continued shortage of aircraft, the RAF squadrons operated in the North Sea and the Channel in small groups, each aircraft quartering its own sector. These missions were known as *Rovers* and were to prove an uneconomical method of using such vulnerable aircraft.

In September, six Beauforts of No. 22 Squadron, led by Flight Commander Francis, made a night torpedo attack on shipping assembled at Cherbourg, However, *en route* to the attack they ran into heavy cloud, which split the formation. The original plan had been for the Beauforts to attack in three waves, which would cross the harbour in pairs from the east, north and west, and it was hoped that the ships would be silhouetted by fires started by preceding altitude attacks. Four aircraft made drops, one was shot down over the target zone and another got lost and turned back. Reconnaissance next morning showed that one merchant ship had been hit and damaged in this assault.

Similar missions continued throughout the autumn of 1940 with a few victories for the bombers but No. 22 Squadron suffered very heavy losses in the process. One of the most gallant exploits of this famous unit was that carried out on the

Another Italian victim of the Swordfish torpedo attack on Taranto. *Author*

and flares. Lieutenant Commander K. Williamson led the first wave and they arrived over the harbour at 11.00 p.m. as the flare markers were released. A formidable balloon barrage and scattered anti-aircraft fire met them but, despite this, all the attacks were pressed home and only one Swordfish was destroyed.

At midnight the second wave reached Taranto, by now a scene of some disorganisation. Again, anti-aircraft fire was intense but uncoordinated and these Swordfish also carried out their strikes perfectly, once more losing only a single aircraft to the defences. The result was a famous victory. Twenty-one obsolete aircraft had, in six and half hours' flying time, in Admiral Cunningham's words, 'inflicted more damage upon the Italian fleet than was inflicted upon the German High Seas Fleet in the daylight action of the Battle of Jutland'. Subsequent reconnaissance showed the extent of the damage these gallant young crews had wrought in the Italian's own front parlour. Three of the six battleships had been torpedoed. The *Cavour* took one hit and sank, the *Duilio* took one hit and sank by the bows and the brand new *Littorio* was hit by no fewer than three torpedoes and sunk, although she was later raised and repaired. In addition, the heavy cruiser *Trento* and the destroyers *Libeccio* and *Pessango* had been hit and two naval auxiliaries sunk. On shore, several oil storage tanks were burnt out and seaplane hangars bombed.

Little wonder then that Admiral Cunningham signalled the returning carrier with the understatement, '*Illustrious* manoeuvre well executed'. This superb attack will be remembered as the Fleet Air Arm's equivalent to the Battle of Britain. It was a master stroke at a time when the course of the war had taken a far from happy turn for Britain. As well as vindicating the torpedo-bomber concept once and for all, Taranto also marked the greatest achievement of the obsolete little 'Stringbags', although they had yet other glorious chapters to write in the pages of maritime history.

Throughout 1940 and 1941, the British torpedo bombers working from the island of Malta were mainly Fleet Air Arm units. The first of these was No. 830 Squadron formed on 22 July 1940, by Swordfish of No. 767 Training Squadron. Never at a greater strength than two dozen aircraft at any time, these Swordfish played an important part in harassing the Axis supply lines to North Africa. In a nine-month period they despatched an average of no fewer than 50,000 tons of Italian shipping, and in one month alone they sank 98,000 tons.

In October 1941, these Swordfish were joined and gradually replaced by Albacores of No. 828 Squadron, which began operations that month and continued to operate from Malta until July 1943. Typical of their missions was that carried out in July 1942 when nine Albacores of No. 828 Squadron flew from Dekheila to attack a convoy off Tripoli with secret refuelling from Bombay transports some 250 miles behind Axis lines en route.

The first RAF torpedo bomber unit to operate in this theatre of war was No. 39 Squadron equipped with Beauforts, which arrived in the desert towards the end of the year. Co-operating with the Albacores from Malta and Egypt, three Beauforts

A mixed team of soldiers, sailors and airmen combine to arm and check the loading of a torpedo into the bomb-bay of an RAF Blenheim IV in Malta. *IWM*

were sent against a large Italian convoy on 23 January 1942. They managed to score a hit on the 14,000-ton liner *Victoria* and the Albacores later finished her off.

On 13 April, however, another aircraft strike against a large convoy crossing the central Mediterranean turned into a massacre for the RAF. Nine Beauforts were despatched, including two from No. 22 Squadron on their way through Egypt to the Far East. They were to fly from Egypt, attack the convoy and then land at Malta. Four Beaufighters were sent as fighter escort. They found the convoy heavily defended by fighters. They managed to attack and claimed two hits, but they were harassed all the way to Malta and seven of the Beauforts were lost, only two badly damaged planes reaching the island.

No. 39 Squadron was re-equipped and based at Sidi Barrani and No. 217 Squadron was flown into Malta to commence operations in June. At dawn on 15 June 1942, the Italian battleships *Littorio* and *Vittorio Veneto*, two heavy and two light cruisers with twelve destroyers, left Taranto to attack an Allied convoy to Malta. To attack this formidable force, the British torpedo bomber forces were far from strong. Nos 39 and 217 Squadrons equipped with Beauforts and four Wellingtons were fitted for night torpedo bombing. Of these, only one was able to attack, at 3.40 a.m. on 16 June, through a thick smokescreen and her two torpedoes ran wide.

Beauforts of No. 217 Squadron from Malta were a little more accurate. Leaving Malta at 4.00 p.m., they located the Italians at dawn and immediately attacked. The first three aircraft chose the pair of 8-inch cruisers as their targets and Pilot Officer Aldridge scored a single hit on the *Trento*. The remaining six aircraft launched their torpedos against the battleships and pressed in with outstanding bravery to within 200 yards of their giant opponents, crossing their decks with feet to spare. Despite their claims to have scored two hits on each of the Italian battleships, they had, in fact, missed completely. The Italian fleet was not stopped or even slowed down. Only two of the crews involved had ever before taken part in a real attack on enemy warships before this operation.

Beauforts of No. 39 Squadron attacked the Italian fleet after a high-level Liberator attack had claimed to have scored twenty-three hits but in reality had scored only one, which did no serious damage at all. Of the twelve Beauforts despatched, only five, led by Pat Gibbs, ever reached the Italian ships because they were intercepted on the way by German fighters. Of these five all managed to drop their torpedos at long range but again no hits were scored.

Not put off by their earlier failures, both No. 217 Squadron and the Wellingtons attacked again later, as the Italian fleet was returning to Taranto. The Beauforts failed to find their target but Pilot Officer Hawes of No. 38 Squadron attacked through thick cloud and gained absolute surprise. Launching both his torpedoes at the *Littorio*'s port bow, he scored one hit. Again, despite claims, the battleship was not seriously affected by this; it did not even reduce her speed and the Italians reached harbour on 16 June.

This lack of a decisive result dogged the squadrons based at Malta during June and July 1942. On 20 June, a strike by twelve of No. 217's Beauforts against a small Axis convoy was a complete failure. One aircraft turned back, two were intercepted *en route* to the target and the other nine failed to find the convoy. The next day nine Beauforts led by Squadron Leader Lynn hit with four torpedoes, and sank, the 7600-ton *Reichenfels*, at a cost of three aircraft destroyed and the others all damaged.

Twelve Beauforts of No. 39 Squadron attacked two merchant vessels on 24 June, damaging one cargo ship, at a cost of three aircraft. This convoy was reassembled and attacked several times by torpedo-equipped Wellingtons with no decisive result. A strike on 4 July by eight Beauforts, four of which turned back, resulted in damage to one ship of the three and the loss of three more Beauforts. On 21 July, of six Beauforts from No. 86 and No. 217 Squadrons yet another three aircraft were lost after causing damage to a small merchant vessel.

Better results were achieved on 17 August, when the 8300-ton *Rosalina Pilo* was sunk off Lampedusa. On 20 and 21 August the 7800-ton tanker *Posarica* was destroyed with the loss of three Beauforts. On 27 August the 1500-ton *Delphi* was destroyed, and Wellingtons sank the 5400-ton *Istria*. On 30 August nine Beauforts struck the 5000-ton *San Andrea* and sank her, while the 5000-ton tanker *Proserpina* and the 6000-ton *Tergestea* were both sunk on 26 October 1942.

Italian Operations

On 2 April 1941, two SM.79s of 34 *Gruppo* attacked British shipping at Crete and sank the 5325-ton merchant vessel *Homefield*. On 18 April, the tanker *British Science* was torpedoed by Cimicchi of the same unit. In May three SM.79s hit the steamer *Rawnsley*. During the battle for Crete, 281 *Squadriglia* made many attacks in co-operation with the *Luftwaffe* upon Cunningham's fleet defending that island. But the only achievement was that of sinking the already damaged destroyer *Hereward* after she had been hit by Stukas. In August that year, an attack by three SM.79s piloted by Buscaglia, Graziani and Forzinetti resulted in a hit on the netlayer *Protector* by Graziani but she did not sink.

On 20 August 1941, two of 281's aircraft severely damaged the tanker *Turbo* (4782 tons) while the next day they attacked a destroyer off Alexandria and claimed a single hit. On 13 October, three of 281's torpedo bombers made a daylight attack on the British Battle Fleet west of Alexandria, Cesare and Faggioni attacking the battleship *Queen Elizabeth*, while Cimicchi pressed home his attack against the *Barham*. He thought that he had hit her but this claim was not substantiated and a

An Allied freighter burning and sinking following sustained torpedo bomber attacks by Italian Savoia Marchetti SM.79 units on the Malta-bound convoy *Pedestal* in August 1942. *Ufficio Storico, Roma*

An Italian Savoia Marchetti SM.79 three-engined, land-based torpedo bomber swoops over her blazing and sinking victim after another successful attack on a Malta-bound convoy in 1942. *Ufficio Storico, Roma*

Allied freighters on fire and sinking between Cape Serrat and Ras Zelib, after attacks by Italian Savoia Marchetti SM.79 Aerosilurante units on the Pedestal convoy. *Ufficio Storico, Roma*

month later she fell victim to the German submarine *U-331* in the same waters.

On 24 October, Focacci sank the solitary freighter *Empire Guillemot* west of Galita Island, as she was trying to slip through to Malta. Against the heavily escorted Malta convoys the Italians also had some successes, although losses increased as the size of the escort grew with each operation.

On 10 January 1941, attacks by SM.79s at sea level upon the *Illustrious* during Operation *Excess* played a major part in luring away her defending fighters and thus leaving her open to the concentrated attack by the Stukas who heavily damaged her.

On 23 July, a force of seven SM.79s attacked the Malta convoy *Substance* heading east from Gibraltar and achieved absolute surprise. Their torpedoes struck the

A German Heinkel He.111-T low over the water after an attack on a freighter which subsequently blew up and sank in the Sicilian Narrows during the attack on the Pedestal convoy in 1942. *Gerd Stamp*

cruiser *Manchester* in the engine room and disabled three of her four engines. She was towed back to Gibraltar by the destroyers. In the same attack another torpedo hit the destroyer *Fearless* aft in her oil fuel tanks. Ablaze, the crippled destroyer lost her way and later had to be sunk. The next day the already damaged merchant ship *Sydney Star* was attacked by two SM.79s, which pressed home their assault to such an extent that one flew between her masts. They scored a single torpedo hit but the ship still reached Malta.

On 27 September 1941, the *Halberd* convoy from Gibraltar to Malta was attacked by twelve BR.20 torpedo bombers. They lost four of their number without scoring any hits. A further attack was made by these aircraft, six pressing in across the destroyer screen and launching their torpedoes at the *Nelson* at mast-head height. Although the great vessel skilfully avoided two of these torpedoes, a third hit her in her bows, ten feet below the waterline, and reduced her speed considerably; but she stayed in line. Further torpedo bomber assaults were made by moonlight that night and the 12,000-ton freighter *Imperial Star* was hit and later sank.

In 1942, the convoys got larger as Malta's plight became more desperate, the Royal Navy's escort grew heavier, but the Axis forces, battleships, cruisers, destroyers, E-boats, dive and torpedo bombers also vastly increased to their wartime peak. The result was several very fierce encounters. By June the position was extreme and Britain decided to run in two convoys, one from each end of the Mediterranean. From the west would come *Harpoon* and from the east, *Vigorous*. The Axis replied by sending out strong naval and air forces against both convoys and the result was a massacre. Seventeen merchant ships sailed and only two arrived at Malta. However, the contribution made by the Italian torpedo bombers was limited. In an attack on *Harpoon* Buscaglia hit the already damaged destroyer *Bedouin* with a torpedo and sank her, while the *Liverpool* was hit and towed home for the second time in the war.

The last and greatest of all the Malta convoy operations was *Pedestal*, which took place in August 1942 from the west only. I have already written at length to describe this famous battle, and so here will only summarise the part played by the torpedo bombers (see *Pedestal; The convoy that saved Malta*, Peter C. Smith, Goodall, Manchester, 2003). Fourteen merchant ships escorted by two battleships, three aircraft carriers, seven cruisers and two dozen destroyers formed the convoy. The Axis torpedo bomber forces consisted of fifty-nine SM.79s from 130 *Gruppo*, 254, 255, 278 and 281 Squadrons, sixteen SM.84s of 130 *Gruppo* and six Heinkel He.111s from 11/G.26, which had been undergoing training at Grosseto.

The first torpedo bomber attack was by the six German aircraft at dusk on 11 August against the *Victorious*, without result. The major air assault took place the next day and at 12.40 p.m. the first wave of bombers reached the convoy. These were ten S.84s of 132 *Stormo* carrying *Motobombas*. These were dropped in the path of the ships to force them to turn away, thus opening up the convoy's defensive ranks and enabling the torpedo bombers to penetrate the screen of warships to reach the merchantmen. It was a good plan but lack of co-ordination resulted in the subsequent waves arriving too late to take advantage of this. They were met with heavy anti-aircraft fire and the fleet's fighters, with the result that no hits were scored. One SM.79 and two SM.84s were lost in this attack.

The second assault took place at 6.00 p.m. and, again, although co-ordination was better the only hit scored by the Italian torpedo bombers, twenty-two of which took part, was that scored on the destroyer *Foresight*. She was struck aft in her steering compartment and after a long attempt to tow her home she had to be sunk.

At dusk, the six Heinkels returned to attack twice, hitting the convoy as it tried to force the narrows under heavy submarine attack. Two He.111s caught the steamer *Deucalion* off the Cani Rocks and, coasting in with their engines cut, achieved surprise, hitting her with two torpedoes. She blew up and later sank. Another Heinkel put a torpedo into the *Brisbane Star* but she managed after a while to carry on independently and reached Malta. Another torpedo from one of the German aircraft struck the *Clan Ferguson*, which blew up with a tremendous explosion and sank with heavy loss of life.

Many merchant ships were badly damaged by E-boat attacks during the night and in the morning the Axis torpedo bombers were kept busy finishing off these unfortunates. The *Wairangi*, *Santa Elisa* and *Almeria Lykes* were sent to the bottom of the sea. But determined attacks by SM.79s against the lone tanker *Ohio* failed, due in great part to the spirited defence put up by her escorts, one of which, the destroyer *Pathfinder*, steamed head-on into a formation of six SM.79s and drove them off. Thus ended the largest air/sea battle of the Mediterranean.

British Operations in the Atlantic

The faithful old Swordfish continued to operate during 1941 and into 1942 in their original torpedo role and added yet more laurels to their enviable record. In the North Atlantic in May 1941, the great German battleship *Bismarck* broke out and, after destroying the *Hood* and damaging the *Prince of Wales*, looked certain to reach France and safety before the Home Fleet could stop her. Everything depended on the Swordfish squadrons embarked in the brand new carrier *Victorious* and Force H's carrier *Ark Royal*.

At 10.00 p.m. on 24 May, Lieutenant Commander E. Esmonde led nine Swordfish from *Victorious* and flew through rain-squalls to make a night attack on their target.

At 11.27 p.m. they made radar contact and sighted *Bismarck*. They attacked soon after midnight and managed to score a single hit, but as this was on her amidships armoured belt it caused no damage.

Contact was then lost for a considerable time but when it was re-established only the *Ark Royal* stood between the *Bismarck* and sanctuary. At 2.50 p.m. on 25 May, fourteen Swordfish left *Ark Royal*'s flight deck, which was rearing and plunging in heavy seas. At 3.50 p.m. they made their attacks, but against the light cruiser *Sheffield* of Force H and not the *Bismarck*. Fortunately the cruiser avoided the torpedoes and held her fire. She was also able to notify her attackers that their torpedoes were exploding prematurely due to a fault in their magnetic pistols. The second strike had these replaced by contact pistols. It says very little for the warship identification ability of even seasoned Fleet Air Arm pilots when they could mistake a 9000-ton cruiser with twin funnels and triple mountings for the 42,000-ton single-funnelled, twin mountings, *Bismarck*, especially when *Sheffield* had accompanied them at sea for many weeks.

Naval armourers load a torpedo onto a Fairey Swordfish aboard a carrier. *IWM*

The second wave left the *Ark Royal* at 7.10 p.m. and comprised fifteen Swordfish. These Swordfish from Nos 810, 818 and 820 Squadrons were led by Lieutenant Commander T.P. Coode. They first located the *Sheffield*, which then carefully redirected them to the *Bismarck*. They attacked at 10.47 p.m. and scored two hits during the next thirty-eight minutes. One was on the armoured belt; the other was aft, a vital hit, which disabled her steering gear and jammed her rudders. She was now doomed and went down under the guns of the Home Fleet the next day.

Esmonde and the Swordfish of 825 Squadron also featured in the last gallant torpedo bomber attack mounted by the 'Stringbags'. The *Ark Royal* was sunk by a single U-boat torpedo in November 1941 and No. 825 Squadron was re-formed under Esmonde at Manston in Kent. Here they were held in readiness for a night attack on the battle-cruisers *Scharnhorst* and *Gneisenau* and the heavy cruiser *Hipper* if they should run up the Channel as was expected. The Channel dash did in fact take place, but by day and not by night. Esmonde and his six obsolete torpedo bombers were flung in against them on 12 February 1942.

They located the three German giants ten miles off Ramsgate, surrounded by escorting warships and with the sky black with the *Luftwaffe*. Nonetheless, the six Swordfish, with minimum fighter cover, attacked although they knew that their chances were just about nil. They attacked in line astern and all were shot down within a few minutes by the warships' anti-aircraft guns, without scoring any hits. Esmonde was awarded a posthumous Victoria Cross. Of the eighteen pilots and crew, only five survived the attack.

The RAF then sent in what torpedo bombers it had. Squadron Leader George Taylor DFC led seven of No. 217 Squadron's Beauforts against the German ships. Two failed to find the target, one was shot down and the others attacked bravely but did not hit. Nine of No. 42 Squadron's Beauforts also attacked without result, as did 242 conventional bombers of the RAF's Bomber Command. Of the bombers, only thirty-nine actually found the German ships and they did not hit with a single bomb. The final torpedo-bomber attack was mounted by twelve Beauforts of Nos 86, 22 and 217 Squadrons led by Wing Commander Charles Flood; but they also failed to locate the German ships, which reached Germany with only mine damage.

The comparative failure of the slow Beaufort in this and many other attacks, coupled with heavy losses, led ultimately to its replacement and the introduction into the RAF of the Beaufighter as a torpedo aircraft. The Mark 1C Beaufighter, which was powered by two 1425-horsepower Bristol Hercules XI engines, was fitted with torpedo installations. When equipped with this aircraft, the RAF was finally to play an effective role against shipping.

The Swordfish had a record without equal in the torpedo bomber role but after the massacre in the Channel in 1942 it was obvious that this old aircraft had had its day as a torpedo bomber. But its duties were far from complete and the Swordfish became used as general-purpose anti-submarine aircraft, armed with rockets and depth charges and operating from escort carriers in the Atlantic and on the Russia convoys. The Swordfish carried on well past D-Day before being completely phased out of service.

German Operations

As we have seen earlier, the *Luftwaffe* was backward in developing torpedo bombing and with ample evidence of its effectiveness the air force's plans had to be re-cast. By 1941, the *Luftwaffe* had started to take interest in the torpedo bomber but its efforts were not welcomed by the Navy. Much of the data already gained on the use of aerial torpedoes was held back by the Navy, the Technical Office was not assisted and independent work with private firms was hindered.

Nonetheless the *Luftwaffe* set up a torpedo-bombing school at Grossenbrode, and, by the autumn of 1941, had reached the conclusion that the Heinkel He.111 and the Junkers Ju.88 were both suitable types for torpedo-bombing. Initial work was commenced with the He.111-H6 variant and this became the main workhorse of the *Luftwaffe*'s torpedo-bomber force.

The He.111-H6 could be adapted to carry two F4B torpedoes externally. The *Luftwaffe* was so confident of its suitability that several of these aircraft were sent out to Athens to operate in the Eastern Mediterranean. However, owing to lack of torpedoes or non-arrival of the warheads, these operations had to be abandoned.

In December 1941, a direct demand was made by Göring that the *Luftwaffe* should assume control of aerial torpedo development in both Germany and Italy, and further, that experimental stations should be set up, naval personnel absorbed and a Commissioner appointed to control all aspects. Permission was immediately granted.

The anti-shipping expert Harlinghausen became the Commissioner and plans were made to set up a force of 230 torpedo bombers. As the Grossenbrode base in the Baltic was wintered in, the training and development unit was moved down to Grossetto, south of Leghorn in Italy. There, training could continue at full speed and close liaison with the *Aerosilurante* could be maintained.

The crack anti-shipping squadrons of KG.26, based in Norway, were the first units to be converted to this new role. By the end of April 1942, the first twelve crews of I/KG.26 had been trained and were equipped with He.111-H6s. They were based at the specially built airfields of Banak and Bardufoss in north Norway, where they could menace convoys to Russia. The whole of I/KG.26, equipped with forty-two

The staffel aircrew pose in front of their He.115 seaplane at this German base early in the war. The photo gives an indication of the sheer size of the aircraft. *Stein via James V. Crow*

aircraft, was ready by June 1942, while III/KG.26 was undergoing conversion to the Junkers Ju.88A 17 for a similar role. By July 1942, some forty-two Heinkels and thirty-three Junkers, these latter based at Rennes in France, were ready for operations. In the remarkably short time of eight months the *Luftwaffe* had, from scratch almost, developed the most effective torpedo bomber striking force in Europe.

The first successful torpedo bomber attack that this powerful and confident new arm of the *Luftwaffe* made was that carried out against the ill-fated convoy PQ.17 when it was still unbroken and strongly guarded and heading for Soviet Russia packed with arms, ammunition and equipment. An earlier attack, on PQ.16, had shown that high-level dive-bombing by orthodox Ju.88s coupled with the launching of torpedoes from 30 feet, the normal launching height, would greatly upset the convoy escorts. Therefore, these combined attacks were practised at length while the actual torpedo-bombing technique was developed. The torpedo bombers were to approach in a wide line abreast, known as the 'Golden Comb' (*Goldene Zange*), launching all their missiles together in a twilight assault with the convoy silhouetted against the setting sun.

A Heinkel He.115 B-2 seen during take-off and landing trials on ice in 1940. *Franz Selinger*

PQ.17 consisted of thirty-four merchant ships with a strong escort of destroyers and lesser ships, a covering cruiser squadron and the Home Fleet, with two battleships, a carrier, cruisers and destroyers, in far distant support. It was the German Navy's torpedo bombers of 1/906 Squadron, however, that made the first impact on this doomed convoy. At 4.50 p.m. on 3 July one of the floatplanes that had been shadowing the ships cut its engines and at a height of only 30 feet glided gently in over the convoy and released its two torpedoes before soaring safely away. One of the torpedoes struck the 7197-ton *Christopher Newport*, which was promptly abandoned and was later finished off by a submarine.

The afternoon of 4 July saw the *Luftwaffe* make its initial strike. All three *Staffeln* of I/KG.26 took part in this assault from Bardufoss, a total of twenty-three Heinkels. The Ju.88s of KG.30 were to co-operate with a bombing attack. This assault was led by the commander of the I/KG.26's 3rd *Staffel*, Captain Eicke. The twenty-three Heinkels attacked in two waves and were opposed by massed fire, most of it wild, from the convoy, and steadier and more accurate fire from the escorting warships. None of this was very effective but with the convoy at the time was the US destroyer *Wainwright*, which was better equipped than British vessels for air attack. This ship, like the *Pathfinder* during *Pedestal*, took the novel but wise course of steaming directly out towards the incoming torpedo bombers to break them up.

The wave she thus engaged consisted of about ten aircraft and of these, only one, piloted by Lieutenant Kaumeyer, bored in over the destroyer and past her to launch one torpedo before being shot down.

On the starboard quarter of the convoy the other Heinkels were allowed to press in toward their targets, some launching at 6000 yards' range while others, including Eicke, pressed even closer. These, the outstanding example being Lieutenant Hennemann, crossed right through the convoy. For a total loss of three aircraft, hits were made on three ships: *William Hooper*, (7177 tons), *Navarino* (4841 tons) and *Azerbaigen* (6114 tons).

The success of this attack led the *Luftwaffe* at the time (and some British writers since) to assume that this torpedo bomber attack had caused the break up of PQ.17. However, it was the threat of the *Tirpitz*, which had briefly put to sea, that did this, but nonetheless it was a gallant debut.

An attack on a convoy off the Scilly Isles on the night of 3 August by the Rennes aircraft was not such a success, but the work of II/ KG.26 against *Pedestal* as already described the same month was outstanding. However, the greatest *Luftwaffe* victory was once again against a Russia-bound convoy. This took place on 17 October 1942 when the convoy PQ.18 came under attack. The *Luftwaffe* units in Norway had reached a total strength of ninety-two aircraft with the arrival in the zone of III/KG.26 with a strength of thirty-five Ju.88s. Warnings had already been received that PQ.18 would be accompanied by an escort carrier with single-engined fighters

The Blohm und Voss BV.140. *Franz Selinger*

embarked. This would greatly add to the torpedo bombers' problems. The decision was taken therefore that this carrier should be made one of the prime targets of the attacks. Should she be sunk or damaged the rest of the convoy would fall easily.

In fact, the Royal Navy was equally determined to provide the maximum defence for this convoy, and, as in the case of *Pedestal* in the Mediterranean in August, both sides reached their peak strengths at the same time. The carrier provided was the small escort carrier *Avenger*, with Sea Hurricane fighters and Swordfish embarked. A new anti-aircraft cruiser, the *Scylla* with eight 4.5-inch guns, was the flagship of Rear Admiral Bob Burnett and there was a very strong 'Fighting Destroyer Escort' in case German heavy ships should intervene. These, together with the close escort destroyers, amounted to no fewer than eighteen ships. Further heavy anti-aircraft firepower was added with the AA ships *Alynbank* and *Ulster Queen*, while there were additional small escorts, corvettes, minesweepers and trawlers. This massive force was designed to give protection to the convoy, which consisted of forty fully-laden transports bound for Murmansk to supply the Russian armies fighting desperately around Stalingrad.

The German torpedo bombers struck the convoy immediately after the defending Sea Hurricanes had been skilfully lured away by bombing carried out by the Ju.88s of KG.30. The result was devastating. For the first time the 'Golden Comb' was used to maximum effect and the British escorts described their first appearance at 3.00 p.m. in line abreast, thirty feet above the water, as like 'a huge flight of nightmare locusts'.

The convoy was in block formation of ten columns each of four ships, although there were already some gaps where the U-boats had been active in the preceding days. The torpedo bombers attacked from the starboard side of the formation and the Commodore signalled the convoy to carry out an emergency turn of 45 degrees to starboard. The merchantmen, however, were too confused in the face of such an attack to carry this out and remained steaming steadily at right angles to the oncoming bombers.

The torpedo bombers pressed in boldly through an enormous barrage to drop their missiles with deadly accuracy. Only five bombers fell to the massed fire of the escorting warships and aircraft. The others released their torpedoes, some seventy-four in all, and were soon over the horizon as their missiles struck home.

Of the seven ships in the two starboard columns, six were hit, one blowing up with, a colossal explosion, the others emitting great clouds of steam and smoke as they lurched beneath the ocean. Further torpedoes passed into the heart of the massed ranks of steamers and two more ships went down. It was a disaster, for at a cost of five aircraft the men of KG.26 had, in eight minutes, sunk eight heavily laden steamers, a quarter of the convoy. The ships destroyed in. this attack were the

The air and ground crews of the four-engined He.117A-5 of II/KG40 muster at their main base at Boreaux-Merigna in 1944 pending another strike in the Bay of Biscay. *Rosch via James V. Crow*

Empire Beaumont, *Empire Stevenson*, *John Penn*, *Wacosta*, *Afrikander*, *Oregonian*, *Macbeth* and *Sukhona*.

Two further attacks by nine then twelve torpedo bombers later that day did not score any further hits and two bombers were destroyed. It was plain that the first attack was the high-water mark of the *Luftwaffe*'s efforts. Two more attacks were mounted on 14 August by twenty and twenty-five torpedo bombers, most of which concentrated on the *Avenger* and other escorts. But her Sea Hurricanes managed to intercept them this time and with the loss of three of their own number, and aided by the warship's barrage, they claimed to have destroyed a further twenty-one Heinkels and Junkers. Despite this the torpedo bombers again got through to the convoy and hit the ammunition ship *Mary Luckenbach* in the starboard column, which blew up with a great explosion.

On 15 August, only small attacks were made, without effect, by ordinary bombers. On 16 August a determined assault by a mere twelve of KG.26's aircraft penetrated right into the convoy and hit the *Kentucky*, which was later finished off by dive-bombers. The ten ships destroyed in these October battles marked the swansong of the *Luftwaffe*'s torpedo bomber forces in the Arctic as in November they were sent to Cagliari. The orders, which came through to withdraw to bases at Grosseto and Catania on 2 November, were given because it was thought that there would be more success attacking shipping in the warm waters of the Mediterranean than in northern waters. The transfer of the *Gruppen* took only five to nine days, and one *Staffel* managed it in forty-eight hours.

Japanese and United States Operations

When Japan entered World War II in December 1941, the United States Pacific Fleet, moored at Pearl Harbor on the Hawaiian island of Oahu, was the only Allied force that posed any serious threat to Japanese ambitions. On 7 December, an armada launched from the six big aircraft carriers of Vice-Admiral Nagumo's *Kido Butai* (Striking Force) carried out a devastating surprise attack on the eight old battleships of the US fleet, which were still at their peacetime dispositions on that Sunday morning.

The first wave of 183 aircraft comprised forty *Kates* led by Lieutenant Commander Shigeharu Murata of the *Akagi*. When the attack had first been planned, the use of torpedo bombers was opposed due to the shallowness of the water at Pearl Harbor but Murata overcame all these difficulties. Achieving complete surprise, the attack was launched at 7.49 a.m. Only five *Kates* were lost in this attack. The 159 Japanese aircraft assigned actually to attack the American fleet left behind them the battleships *Arizona*, *California* and *West Virginia* sunk, *Oklahoma* capsized,

Smoke pours from the stricken USS
Arizona in battleship row after the Japanese
attack on Pearl Harbor in December 1941.
Naval Historical Center, Washington

Torpedoes strike home on US battleships during the Japanese attack on Pearl Harbor. *Naval Historical Center, Washington*

The new British battleship HMS *Prince of Wales* and the elderly battle-cruiser *HMS Repulse* under attack from Japanese Navy land-based bombers off Malaya on 10 December 1941. *IWM HU2763*

'Abandon Ship' – the crew of the battleship HMS *Prince of Wales* take to the lifeboats as the ship sinks after the Japanese bombing and torpedo attack. *IWM HU2675*

and the *Nevada, Maryland, Pennsylvania* and *Tennessee* damaged, along with three light cruisers, three destroyers and many auxiliaries.

Within three days the Japanese Navy achieved what no other air force of any nation had done; the destruction of two capital ships at sea. This came about when British Admiral Tom Philips bravely sortied north from Singapore into the South China Sea with the new battleship *Prince of Wales*, the ancient battle-cruiser *Repulse* and three destroyers in order to destroy reported Japanese invasion fleets heading towards Malaya. The RAF had pulled its fighters back to the island and the fleet had no carrier. Even so, Philips knew that the nearest bases available to the Japanese were those handed over by the Vichy authorities around Saigon, 400 nautical miles

An Imperial Japanese Navy Nakajima B5N2 Type 97 Attack bomber, carrying a standard aerial torpedo, takes off from a Japanese carrier. The Kate formed the mainstay of the Japanese carrier-born torpedo arm for most of the war, but suffered heavy losses. *Author*

away, and, it is said, Philips believed that no torpedo bomber in the world at that time had such a range!

The British squadron was sighted heading north on the afternoon of 9 December and the message was received at Saigon at 4.00 p.m. that day. The 22nd Air Flotilla of the 11th Air Fleet was based here. The *Genzan* Squadron under the command of Captain Sonokawa consisted of G4M2 *Betty* bombers and they were loading up in preparation for an attack on Singapore. They hastily rearmed with torpedoes and took off at 6.00 p.m. After quartering the likely course of the British ships, the *Genzan* Squadron returned at midnight without sighting them.

At 6.00 a.m. ten *Genzan* Squadron *Bettys* armed with bombs took up the hunt again. At 7.00 a.m. the main striking force, of twenty-seven high-level bombers and sixty-one torpedo bombers, *Bettys* and *Nells*, from the *Genzan*, *Mikoro* and *Kanoya* Squadrons, also set off to attack the two British heavy ships. At 11.00 a.m. on 10 December they were sighted, and half an hour later the assault started. The torpedo bombing analysis shows that the *Genzan* Squadron dropped seven torpedoes against *Repulse*, of which four were hits; the *Kanoya* Squadron launched twenty torpedoes, with ten hits; and the *Mikoro* Squadron hit with four of their seven torpedoes against the elderly battle-cruiser.

Against the brand-new *Prince of Wales* were dropped nine torpedoes from the *Genzan* Squadron (four of which were claimed as hits) and six from the *Kanoya*

Squadron (four of which were claimed hits). Although the numbers of hits actually made was far fewer than those claimed, it mattered little for the result was the same. A surprise for the British was that the Japanese torpedoes were dropped, and ran perfectly true, from a height of 300 to 400 feet. Current British practice had been for an approach to be made at 30 to 40 feet. This high approach nullified much of the close-range anti-aircraft fire.

Almost at once two torpedoes struck home close together aft on the *Prince of Wales*, totally disabling her propellers. From that fateful moment she was doomed – unable to move she had to sit and take it as torpedo after torpedo slammed into her. The older *Repulse* made a fight of it, and steaming at high speed, managed to evade several attacks. Finally, however, a pincer movement saw her trapped and several torpedoes hit her. She had hardly any armour and her bulges were old and obsolete, offering little in the way of true protection. She, too, was mortally struck.

The *Repulse* went down at 12.33 p.m. and the *Prince of Wales* sank with Admiral Philips at 1.20 p.m. The cost to the Japanese Navy was a mere four aircraft. Having sunk the American and British battleships with a combination of high-level, dive- and

Japanese strike aircraft about to take off for a major attack. Zeke fighters, Val dive bombers and Kate torpedo planes can be seen on the carrier's flight deck. *Naval Historical Center, Washington*

torpedo-bombing attacks, the Japanese Navy moved south-west, quickly overrunning Allied positions. After their surface fleet defeated an Allied squadron in the Java Sea, Nagumo's carriers sortied into the Indian Ocean and their dive-bombers sank the carrier *Hermes*, the heavy cruisers *Cornwall* and *Dorsetshire*, the destroyer *Vampire* and others. *Nells* from shore bases despatched the American seaplane carrier *Langley* south of Java.

In these victories the torpedo bombers were not called upon to act other than as orthodox level-bombers. To protect their southern flank and prepare a springboard for the invasion of Australia, the Japanese thrust towards New Guinea and this resulted in the first carrier-to-carrier air/sea battle of the war, the Battle of the Coral Sea, which took place on 7/8 May 1942. The Japanese had three carriers available, the large *Shokaku* and *Zuikaku* and the small *Shoho*. The Allies had a cruiser force and the carriers *Lexington* and *Yorktown*.

The US Navy's Grumman TBM Avenger torpedo bomber made its debut at the Battle of Midway in June 1942, flying from land bases they suffered heavy loss. The aircraft went on to redeem itself in subsequent carrier battles in the Pacific and also served with the Royal Navy (initially as the Tarpon) in the European, East Indian and Pacific theatres of World War II. *IWM A19903*

At 6.10 a.m. on 7 May, the large Japanese carriers launched a striking force, which included twenty-four *Kates*, against a US force. In the subsequent assault the oiler *Neosho* and the destroyer *Sims* were sunk quickly by bombs and torpedoes. The Americans struck back with torpedo and dive-bombing attacks on the *Shoho*. Ten Devastators from *Lexington* made their runs at 11.10 a.m. but the Japanese carrier managed to avoid all their missiles. At 11.25 a.m., however, strikes from *Yorktown* bored through what was left of *Shoho*'s defences with terrible effect. Hit by thirteen bombs and seven torpedoes, the carrier went down at 11.36 a.m.

Admiral Takagi now despatched a strike force, which included fifteen *Kate* torpedo bombers, against the American carriers. These aircraft flew off at 4.50 p.m. but they failed to make an attack. The next day, 8 May, at 8.25 a.m. the Japanese launched a ninety-nine-plane combined strike from *Shokaku* and *Zuikaku*. Meanwhile, the *Lexington* had despatched her own bombers. The US aircraft left at 8.15 a.m. but torpedoes launched at *Shokaku* were all at long range and not effective, but she did suffer bomb damage. Twenty Devastators attacked, and three were shot down.

At 11.18 a.m. the Japanese attacked the *Lexington* in two torpedo bomber groups, hitting with a torpedo on each side. *Yorktown* was also attacked but no torpedo hits were obtained, but again the dive-bombers were more successful. *Lexington* later sank but in an incredibly short period the *Yorktown* was patched up sufficiently at Pearl Harbor dockyard to enable her to fight again, and she was ready for the next battle; neither of the Japanese Coral Sea carriers were.

On 4 June 1942 came the decisive Battle of Midway. The Japanese sailed their main strength against this strategic island. Discounting the diversionary attacks against the Aleutians, they had a total of four heavy carriers, with the First Carrier Striking Force, *Akagi*, *Kaga Hiryu* and *Soryu*, plus the light carriers with the Main Body, the *Hoshu* and *Zuiho*. Each of the four big carriers had aboard twenty-one *Kate* torpedo bombers, commanded respectively by Lieutenant Commander Shigeharu Murata and Lieutenants Ichiro Kitajima, Rokuro Kikuchi and Heijiro Abe.

The first Japanese wave was launched at 4.45 a.m. and consisted of 108 aircraft, which were to strike at Midway Island, but it included no torpedo bombers. The second wave was readied in case the American fleet appeared. This contained a total of thirty-six *Kate* torpedo bombers (eighteen each from the *Akagi* and *Kaga* led by Lieutenant Commander Shigeharu Murata of *Akagi*).

In fact, the Americans were forewarned and ready and waiting. Task Force 16 had the carriers *Hornet* and *Enterprise* under Rear Admiral R.A. Spruance and Task Force 17 had the *Yorktown* under Rear Admiral Fletcher. Both forces were screened only by cruisers and destroyers. They were some two hundred miles north-east of Midway. The first torpedo bomber attack made by the Americans was by six Navy

Avengers and four Army B.26 Marauders from Midway Island, which reached the Japanese fleet at 7.00 a.m. Of the ten, only one Avenger and two Marauders ever returned to Midway and no hits were obtained for their sacrifice. Further attacks by Army B.1 Ts and Marine Dauntless dive-bombers from Midway were equally unsuccessful. The returning Japanese strike force landed at 8.36 a.m. and the US carriers were first sighted at 7.28 a.m. *Akagi* and *Kaga*'s torpedo bombers were being rearmed with bombs for another attack against Midway Island. They had therefore to be struck down yet again and armed once more with torpedoes. But before they could be despatched the American carriers struck hard.

Both *Hornet* and *Enterprise* despatched fourteen torpedo bombers, thirty-three dive-bombers and ten fighters at 7.00 a.m. and began their attacks at 9.30 a.m. The first of these attacks comprised fifteen torpedo bombers of *Hornet*'s VTB-8, led by Lieutenant Commander J.C. Waldron. Set upon by fifty Zero fighters guarding the fleet, every one was shot down and destroyed and of their gallant crews there was only one survivor, Ensign G.H. Gay. They were followed a few minutes later by fourteen torpedo bombers from *Enterprise* and they too took a beating, eleven being shot down, and the torpedoes of the other three all missed their targets. Then came twelve torpedo bombers from *Yorktown* and they also were suffered many losses without result. The sacrifice of the US torpedo bombers at Midway was terrible, of the forty-one aircraft that took part only six returned to their carriers.

But it was not a sacrifice in vain as the torpedo bombers brought the bulk of the defending Japanese Zeros down to sea level. As a result, the Dauntless dive-bombers were able to break through to score a devastating series of direct hits on the fragile wooden flight decks of the *Akagi*, *Kaga* and *Soryu*, all three of which sank with heavy loss of life. Only the *Hiryu* remained to get in a return strike but she only had dive-bombers available. These damaged *Yorktown* in an attack at noon. A second strike of ten *Kates* was sent off at 1.30 p.m. under the command of Lieutenant Joichi Tomonaga. They attacked at 2.40 p.m. and scored two torpedo hits, but only five of the *Kates* returned from the attack. The US dive-bombers then attacked and sank the *Hiryu* and the cruiser *Mikuma*. The battle was now virtually over for the Japanese battleships had been left too far astern to be able to bring their overwhelming firepower into play. It was a major defeat for the Japanese, and a distinct turning point in the Pacific war. But the main part the torpedo bomber had played was to lure the defending Zero fighters down to sea level, which gave the SBDs a free run at dive-bombing. The American torpedo bomber force was almost totally wiped out, only three remaining operational by 7 June.

Despite the appalling debut at Midway, the Grumman Avenger TBF-1 went on to become the most successful carrier-borne torpedo bomber of the war. Designed by William T. Schwendler to replace the Devastator, it was a three-seater, all-metal

US Navy Grumman Avengers queue for take off. *US Navy Official*

A Grumman TBM Avenger makes a practise drop during trials. Initially plagued by inefficient torpedoes that frequently malfunctioned and after a disastrous debut at the Battle of Midway, the Avenger went on to establish itself as a good, reliable airborne launching platform and in conjunction with the Curtiss SB2C Helldiver, formed a deadly duo that crushed the bulk of the Japanese battleship and carrier fleets in 1944 and 1945. *US Navy Official*

monoplane, powered by a single 1850-horsepower Wright Cyclone engine. It had a maximum speed of 259 mph and had a range of 1000 miles. Fitted with a power-operated gun turret, the Avenger could carry a 22-inch torpedo internally. Some 10,000 were built, and of these 1000 were supplied to the Fleet Air Arm under the Lease Lend system. The Royal Navy, however, used this outstanding torpedo bomber as a glide-bomber and anti-submarine aircraft instead of in her true role, and failed to adopt the true dive-bomber types available, like the Dauntless and the Helldiver. As a glide-bomber the Avenger equipped fifteen line squadrons in the Royal Navy. The US Navy used the aircraft mainly in its correct role throughout the war, although it proved itself equally adaptable for minelaying or anti-submarine work with depth-charges, and ship attacks with rockets, as well as bombing.

Chapter Five:

Decline and Abandonment

It was a paradox that, at the very apex of its success in battle, the torpedo bomber started to decline in importance. By assisting in the final destruction of the Japanese Fleet, including the super-battleships *Yamato* and *Musashi*, the torpedo bomber had, almost at a stroke, removed its *raison d'être* and even the subsequent post-war build-up of Soviet Naval power, inexplicably, failed to re-generate its mission requirement. The air-launched, stand-off guided weapon replaced it as the principal, and ultimately, the only air-launched anti-ship weapon[1], although its ability to destroy warships by above-water hits, as with the destroyer *Sheffield* in the Falklands, was only credible because armoured warships by that time no longer existed.

Great Britain

In 1942, the Royal Navy was still heavily reliant on obsolete types like the Swordfish, but they were being phased out, although still operating from escort carriers. In that same year, the Fleet Air Arm was supplied with a monoplane replacement, the Fairey Barracuda. This exceedingly ugly aeroplane was first developed as a replacement for the Albacore in 1937 and made its first flight at the end of 1940, thus becoming the first monoplane torpedo bomber designed for the Royal Navy. The Mark I, of which fewer than thirty were built, did not appear until May 1942. It was not until as late as August 1942, some five years after work had commenced, that the Mark II, which was considered suitable for operational service, was to appear.

It was a three-seater, high-winged monoplane, powered by a 1640-horsepower Rolls-Royce Merlin 32 engine that gave a maximum speed of 228 mph. It could carry a single 1620-pound torpedo externally at a range of 686 miles only. The span was 49 feet 2 inches, the length 35 feet 9 inches and the height 15 feet 4 inches. Although originally designed as a torpedo bomber, it was not an outstanding success in that role. Like the British Avenger, it was used as a dive-bomber during most of its brief wartime service with the Fleet Air Arm — a role for which it was more suited, and one that it performed very well. The most outstanding achievements of the Barracudas were the superb dive-bombing attacks on the *Tirpitz* in 1944. They were employed in the East Indies in the same role, as well as in anti-shipping strikes

[1] See Peter C Smith, *Ship Strike – The History of Air-to Sea Weapons Systems*, Airlife, Shrewsbury 19998

Fairey Barracudas seen in formation. Although designed to perform multiple roles as a torpedo bomber, dive bomber and reconnaissance aircraft, it was hardly ever used in the torpedo dropping role. During its brief appearance in the front line it became more famous as a dive bomber. *IWM*

off the Norwegian coast. For these latter operations, the heavy, clumsy Barracudas were power-assisted off the tiny flight decks by rocket-assisted take-off gear. Rarely used as a torpedo bomber, and inferior by far to the Avenger anyway, the Barracuda was typical of the delayed hybrids that came from British designers of this period.

Not surprisingly then it was superseded in the main attack carriers of the British Pacific Fleet in 1945 by the superior Avenger, large numbers of which became available in 1944/5. These formed the backbone of the British Pacific Fleet's air striking forces in the final drive on Japan. At their peak, Avengers were operational with no fewer than ten Fleet Air Arm squadrons.

The Royal Air Force too was slowly re-equipping. In June 1942, Coastal Command had only two squadrons of torpedo bombers, No. 68 and No. 415.

By 1943 the RAF was finally building up its ant-shipping strike wings with more modern aircraft. Here a Bristol Beaufighter adapted for torpedo bombing stands ready for take-off. IWM

Although it was fully realised that the torpedo was the best weapon against warships, both aircraft and torpedoes remained in short supply. With all the Beauforts operating in the Mediterranean (Nos 42, 86 and 217 Squadrons) at this time, the old Hampden bombers were equipped as torpedo carriers and formed into Nos 144, 415, 455 and 489 Squadrons in July 1942. The Hampdens were slow, sluggish and vulnerable, although they did have the one virtue of reasonable range. The lack of success achieved at this time was so great that the R.A.F. finally equipped the superb Beaufighter to carry torpedoes. During the period January to July 1942, for example, the R.A.F. made 6617 anti-shipping sorties and only achieved the sinking of thirty small ships with the loss of 195 aircraft.

The specially equipped Beaufighters, known as *Torbeaus*, first joined No. 254 Squadron in November 1942 and went into operation with an attack on a German convoy off the Dutch coast on the 20th of that month. The result was an expensive failure. Two squadrons of fighters, Beaufighters and Spitfires, accompanied No. 254 Squadron from its North Coates base on this strike against a fifteen-ship convoy located off the Frisian Islands.

The *Torbeaus* lost three of their number destroyed and four others damaged by flak and the escorting Fw.190s, without scoring a single hit on the convoy. As a direct result of this action the new *Torbeaus* were withdrawn from fighting and did not venture out again until a detailed training programme had been undertaken, which lasted until April 1943.

With the continued heavy losses suffered for slight returns on day operations, the RAF followed the Navy's example by considering night torpedo bombing. For a time during 1942, the Fleet Air Arm made available to Coastal Command several Albacores for this duty. Also, as has already been described, some old Wellington bombers were hastily converted to the torpedo bomber role at Malta, and this was followed by more careful adaptations.

The famous old 'Wimpey' had been Bomber Command's main workhorse for the early part of the war and was now replaced in front-line service by four-engined aircraft. However, it still had good range and capacity for its new task.

The Wellington was a twin-engined, high-winged monoplane. It was powered by two Bristol Pegasus XVIII engines and had a maximum speed of 255 mph with a range of 1325 miles. The Mark VIII was specially developed for Coastal Command operations and was fitted with A.S.V. Mark II search radar. It was known as the 'Stickleback' because of the row of aerials along the aircraft's back. A later mark, the G.R.XI, was intended as a torpedo bomber, carrying the A.S.V. Mark III.

It had a few successes, the most spectacular being the exploits of the No. 44 Squadron Wellingtons during night operations during the abortive Aegean Campaign of the autumn of 1943. On the night of 18 October, four of these

An aerial view of the RAF's Torbeau, a modified Beaufighter, seen sporting D-Day invasion stripes and carrying an aerial torpedo, complete with tail stabilisers. *IWM*

Wellingtons sank the large German steamer *Sinfra*. This was hailed as a great victory as 2000 troops were drowned. Unfortunately, it later turned out that almost all of these were Allied POWs, Italian and Greek, being shipped back to Greece.

The *Torbeaus* were reorganised after their inglorious debut and the RAF's new approach was the sensible one of saturating the defences by using swarms of cannon-firing Beaufighters to knock out the warships' flak defences and then to follow up against the thin-skinned vessels with rockets and torpedoes to deliver the *coup de grâce*. This method was found to work perfectly well in the restricted waters of the North Sea, and by June 1944 the original Strike Wing was joined by a second. With four or five squadrons available for each mission, overwhelming firepower was thus deployed as in the case of the attack by the North Coates and Langham Wings against two ships off Schiermonnikoog on 15 June. The 8000-ton *Amerskerke* and a 4000-ton naval auxiliary vessel were escorted by seven R boats and eleven minesweepers. They were hit by aircraft from Nos 254, 455 and 484 Squadrons acting as anti-flak strikers, by No. 254 Squadron carrying torpedoes and by No. 236 Squadron armed with the new rocket projectiles.

After thirty-two anti-flak Beaufighters had made their passes the four RP-Beaus fired thirty-two rockets, which scored ten hits on the auxiliary ship and eight on the *Amerskerke*. When the ten *Torbeaus* followed, they met no flak and could thus plant two torpedoes into each of the main targets. No aircraft were lost in this assault. This was the greatest of such attacks off Holland but many lesser strikes were made and great carnage was inflicted during the German evacuation of Norway.

The main lesson to be learned from these RAF attacks was not the continued effectiveness of the torpedo, but the overwhelming power of the stand-off rocket.

It could not sink large ships, but then Germany had few of these left. The rocket could, however, wreck their upperworks while small vessels could be sunk by rocket alone. This fact marked the demise of the torpedo in the RAF and it was not widely employed post-war.

Italy and Germany

The SM.79 continued to operate as the main Italian torpedo bomber, though in ever decreasing numbers after the peak of 200 at the end of 1942. Enough details of the actual ships sunk and damaged by the *Aerosilurante* have been given in these pages to confirm that it was a highly effective unit. However, the *Aerosilurante* was credited with a large number of victories that simply did not take place. The list of these non-existent successes is reproduced here, together with the truth.

Ship claimed sunk by SM.79s[2]	Comments and true cause of loss
Eagle (aircraft carrier)	Sunk by German submarine *U-73*
Jaguar (destroyer)	Sunk by German submarine *U-652*
Legion (destroyer)	Bombed three times by Ju.88s and Ju.87s in dock at Malta. Torpedo-bombing not possible.
Southwall (destroyer)	No such ship. Possibly the *Southwold* sunk by mines off Malta.
Kujavik II (destroyer)	No such ship. Possibly Polish *Kujawiak* mined off Malta.
Husky (destroyer)	No such ship. Possibly the *Hasty* sunk by E-boats in Eastern Mediterranean

During the North African landings and the subsequent invasion of Sicily from November 1942 to July 1943, the *Aerosilurante* units co-operated with the German units in frequent attacks on Allied merchant shipping, battle squadrons and ports. At this time the Axis began to learn the lesson already discovered by the Allies and the Japanese, i.e. although the torpedo bomber was the best weapon for use against shipping, its high success rate could only continue while the anti-aircraft armament on ships was relatively weak or the attacking aircraft were in overwhelming numbers. Once strengthened by the additions of 20-mm, and 40-mm automatic cannon in large numbers, the ships were able to make the low approach of the torpedo bomber particularly vulnerable unless swamped by attackers. Aircraft losses when used in penny packets became prohibitive. The Allies and the Japanese learned this lesson early for the Axis and American ships were much better armed than the British in this respect. By 1943, however, the defensive armament of British

---

[2] Most of these untrue claims were promulgated by William Green in this book, *Famous Bombers of World War II*, proving that, although he knew something of aircraft, he knew little or nothing of naval history or ships and had not troubled to verify these statements.

A few Focke Wulf FW.190s were adapted to carry torpedoes toward the latter part of the war.
Archiv Schliephake

ships was starting to catch up slowly with the others and torpedo bomber operations thus became equally expensive for all nations.

Although about 120 German and 200 Italian torpedo bombers were on hand on 8 November 1942, and attacked with great persistence and courage, wastage was very high. The heavy losses of highly trained aircrew suffered throughout November and December were never to be recovered. A principal reason for this was the fuel shortage, which started to cause problems for the Axis at this time. The resulting closure of the training schools meant that the supply of new torpedo bomber crews was reduced to a trickle. A few Focke-Wulf Fw.190s were adapted to carry torpedoes at the end of World War II.

Operational efficiency as well as strength was therefore severely hit. At no time during January and February 1943 did the number of German torpedo bombers available exceed fifty or sixty. By March, it was down to five to ten serviceable aircraft. The Italians fared the same. For example, it was in raids against Allied shipping at Bougie on the night of 11/12 November 1942 that Buscaglia was lost leading his unit.

The results gained by Axis torpedo bombers at this time were far from impressive. The number of victories tailed away with the loss of aircrew. The attacks in which Buscaglia died resulted in the sinking of the AA ship *Tynwald* and heavy damage to the monitor *Roberts*. The sinking of the four large liners the *Cathay*,

Awatea, *Karanja* and *Narkunda* was a greater achievement.

The heavy casualties continued during December with the Axis torpedo bombers being responsible for the sinking of the destroyer *Quentin* off Cape Bon on 2 December, while the cruiser *Argonaut* was hit by two aerial torpedoes that blew away her bow and stern on 14 December. Among the larger liners hit were the *Cameronia* on 22 December and the *Windsor Castle* on 23 February.

A reduction of air attacks was coupled with the drive of the Allied armies along the North African shore until they came to an abrupt halt and back-peddled when they struck the Germans in Tunisia. On 13 March the new circling torpedoes were dropped in Tripoli harbour and two ships were sunk by them.

Between June and December 1943, the official history of the *War at Sea* states that some forty-one ships of 225,450 tons were sunk by aerial attack in the Mediterranean. Wastage of aircrew continued and by 12 June there were only twenty Italian torpedo bombers left, together with a few German aircraft operating from bases in South France. The invasion of Sicily followed in July 1943 and the few torpedo bombers available to the Axis succeeded in hitting and damaging the aircraft carrier *Indomitable*, the monitor *Erebus*, three destroyers and three merchant ships.

Following the Italian surrender in September 1943, some thirty-four SM.79s joined the Italian Co-Belligerent Air Force, although they had little success. The more experienced aircrew joined the Axis *Aviazione della Republica Sociale Italiana* and re-

Stills from a film taken showing a Dornier bomber test-launching a BU.L. 10 torpedo. *Fritz Trenkle*

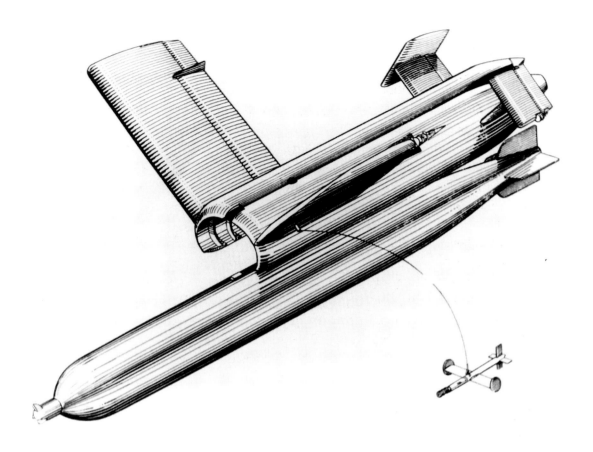

A diagram of the German BU.L.10 torpedo launching device used to keep the missile on track during the drop period. *Archiv Schliephake*

equipped with the S.579 as the *Gruppo Buscaglia*. It was led by Captain Faggioni initially. The Allied landings at Salerno gave an opportunity for dusk attacks by torpedo bombers and no fewer than 155 sorties were made on the night of 8/9 September with another 100 the following night. On 22 January 1944, torpedo bombers sank the destroyer *Janus* at Anzio with heavy loss of life. Captain Faggioni was lost here and replaced by Major Marini.

Attacks by Ju.88 torpedo bombers from South France took place at night three times during April 1944, but had only partial success. On 30 April an attack by sixty Ju.88s against convoy UGS.38 off Algiers resulted in the loss of the US destroyer *Lansdale* and two 7000-ton merchantmen with damage to two others. Countermeasures were so effective that when convoy UGS.40 was attacked by sixty-two Ju.88s on 11 May, although ninety-one torpedoes were dropped, no ships were hit and sixteen of the torpedo bombers were destroyed by AA defences. On

31 May 1944 an attack on convoy KMS.51 by forty Ju.88s sank one ship for the loss of four of the torpedo bombers. On the night of 4/5 June the *Gruppo Buscaglia* made a daring torpedo attack against Gibraltar. The last major torpedo bomber attack of the war in the Mediterranean took place on the night of 1 August when forty bombers struck convoy UGS.48 off Bougie without scoring any hits. After this, the Ju.88s were withdrawn northward into France.

During the final eighteen-month period it was the old Ju.88s that formed the backbone of the Axis torpedo bomber forces, despite the fact that both the Italians and the Germans had sought faster and more modern replacements for them.

Japan and the United States

In the Pacific war, the torpedo bomber featured in conjunction with the dive-bomber in the great carrier battles of 1943/5. The American advance began with the landing on Guadalcanal in the Solomon Islands on 7 August 1942. From then, the Japanese were increasingly on the defensive. On 8 August, for example, an attack mounted by thirty-two Japanese torpedo bombers, on this occasion abandoning the successful high-dropping method and instead using a much more vulnerable wave-skimming approach, met a forewarned defence over the anchorage off the island and seventeen were shot down for the loss of only the single destroyer *Jarvis*. The Japanese 11th Air Fleet at Rabaul attempted to stem the tide of the US advance at a great cost. Other attacks by small task groups never achieved a positive result and losses grew heavier and heavier.

In the Solomon Islands battle of 23 August 1942 the light carrier *Ryuho* was sunk after attacks by Avengers and Dauntless aircraft from the *Enterprise*, but the Japanese return strike failed to inflict any torpedo hits. At the Battle of Santa Cruz on 25 October, the light carrier *Zuiho* was damaged. The *Shokaku* and *Zuikaku* exchanged blows with the *Enterprise* and *Hornet*. The Japanese torpedo bombers led by Lieutenant Commander Shigeharu Murata and Lieutenant Jiichiro Imajuku put two torpedoes into the *Hornet*'s engine room while a third *Kate* crashed into her forward lift. A further torpedo bomber attack suffered heavy losses, but again a damaged *Kate* piled into the destroyer *Smith*, destroying her bridge structure. *Hornet* finally sank but the cost to the Japanese was too heavy for this victory to be decisive and Imajuku and Murata were two veteran torpedo bomber leaders who did not come back.

On 12 November 1943, following a night action off Guadalcanal, the damaged Japanese battleship *Hiei* was caught by torpedo bombers from the *Enterprise* who hit her twice. She stayed afloat, however, and the Avengers returned later to add a further two torpedo hits and the battleship was later scuttled. This same unit from

As the American task forces pressed ever closer to the Japanese mainland, even the Japanese Army became concerned. This is an Army Type 4 Heavy Bomber (Ki-97), given the Allied code name Peggy. The bombers were converted to enable them to carry torpedoes and were sent to attack the Allied fleets, but with little or no success. *Tadashi Nozawa*

Enterprise hit and sank the heavy cruiser *Kinugasa* on 14 November.

On 29 January 1943, Japanese torpedo bombers from Munda hit the heavy cruiser *Chicago* with two torpedoes and the next day sank her with four more at the cost of eleven of the twelve attacking aircraft. In August, the Americans took the Ellis Islands and in November, Tarawa. The only outstanding event by the *Kates* and *Peggys* was a single hit on the carrier *Independence*. The huge American carrier task groups made massive raids against the Marshall Islands and other bases. For example, on 4 December, a hit was scored on the cruiser *Nagara* at Kwajalein. The Eniwetok Islands fell in February 1944, and Truk, the main Japanese fleet base, was raided with heavy losses to the defenders. The great Marianas battle culminated in the Battle of the Philippine Sea on 19 June 1944 when nine Japanese carriers duelled with twelve American. The result was a massacre – 450 aircraft were thrown in by the Japanese and more than 300 were destroyed. US losses were but a tenth of this enormous total and the US torpedo bombers in return sank the carrier *Hiyo* and damaged several other ships. When the Americans landed in the Philippines, the Battle of Leyte Gulf erupted and US torpedo bombers were heavily engaged. The giant battleship *Musashi* was hit by no fewer than twenty-six torpedoes from the swarming Avengers before she sank, while on the same day, 24 October 1944, they hit the cruiser *Myoko*. On 25 October the Avengers torpedoed the cruiser *Tama*, the carrier *Chitose* and the destroyer *Akitsuki*. The carrier *Chiyoda* was next to go down. Further south in this wide-ranging battle, the biggest sea fight of all time, torpedo bombers helped to sink the cruiser *Kumano*.

Again in the north, the carriers *Zuikaku* and *Zuiho* were sunk. The few Japanese torpedo bombers that managed to take part in the action were overwhelmed by the defending fighters and a flak barrage over the American fleet that was larger than that for the entire British Isles. They were wiped out without result, which convinced the Japanese of the futility of further conventional attacks and led to the adoption of *Kamikaze* tactics.

The American fleet, however, still had ample targets for their Avengers and during the closing months of the war, the mighty battleship *Yamato* was sunk with seven or more torpedoes as was her accompanying light cruiser *Yahagi* and four destroyers. The rest of the Japanese fleet was destroyed at anchor due to lack of fuel. Without doubt it was the combination of torpedo bombers and dive-bombers that won the Pacific War at sea. Land-based torpedo-bombing had never been much featured in the US Navy in contrast to the Japanese. One exception was the Navy version of the Mitchell, the North American PBJ.10 Patrol Bomber. It could carry a standard navy torpedo externally and was used in the South West Pacific by Marine flyers.

1945 and After

Orthodox torpedo-bomber development continued in the closing stages of the*
war in both the Royal and the US Navy despite the scarcity of suitable targets. In
Britain the final results were the Blackburn Firebrand and the Fairey Spearfish. The
Firebrand design was begun in 1940 but was not delivered to squadron service until
1945; too late for wartime operations. It was a splendid aircraft – a single-seater
monoplane powered by a 2500-horsepower Bristol Centaurus IX engine, which
gave it a maximum speed of 350 mph with a range of 740 miles. The span was 51
feet 3^1/$_2$ inches, the length was 38 feet 11 inches and the height 14 feet 11 inches.
It could carry a 1850-pound torpedo, externally. It served with No. 827 Squadron

Due to the heavy losses suffered by the torpedo bombers of all nations as the defensive
armament of warships increased massively from 1943 onwards, alternative methods of hitting ship
targets from a safe distance were constantly being sought. The most successful by far were the
Germans and this photo shows the air-launched Blohm und Voss BV 143 rocket bomb boosting
away after launch from its carrying aircraft and being guided to its target by radio control. *Fritz
Trenkle*

* See Peter C Smith, *Ship Strike! –The History of Air-to-Sea Weapons Systems*, Airlife, Shrewsbury, 1998.

aboard *Eagle* in 1952/3. The Fairey Spearfish was a great improvement over the Barracuda but again too late. Powered by a 2320-horsepower Bristol Centaurus engine, it had a maximum speed of only 292 mph but a range of 1036 miles and could carry its torpedo internally for the first time in a Royal Navy torpedo bomber. It never saw production.

The US Navy was in a similar position with the Consolidated TBY-2 Seawolf torpedo bomber. Originally designed by Vought, some 140 were built in 1945 – too late for war service. The Germans also had hopes of making the torpedo bomber a viable proposition again by a combination of new aircraft and 'stand off' torpedoes to overcome the heavy flak problem. Despite extensive trials, however, it was once more a case of too late. As Hitler himself recorded, he had been advised against developing the torpedo bomber pre-war, but now he was asked for it when there was little hope of achieving production. With the abandonment of the South France bases in 1944, the new bombers and new weapons were useless.

Post-war, the two surviving naval powers continued to develop the orthodox carrier-borne torpedo bomber. In Britain the Westland Wyvern and finally the Fairey Gannet finished the story. The Wyvern was seven years' in production. A single-seater monoplane, it was powered by a 4100-horsepower Armstrong-Siddeley Python A.S.P.3 with a speed of 383 mph and a range of 904 miles. It first entered service in May 1953 with No. 813 Squadron and later served aboard *Eagle* and *Albion* including ground attack service during the Suez operation in November 1956. The Gannet was a combined strike and search aircraft. It was a three-seater with a 2950-horsepower Armstrong-Siddeley Double Mamba engine. It could carry two homing torpedoes in its internal bomb bay. It went into service in 1955 and was the last operational torpedo bomber of the Fleet Air Arm.

The US Navy developed the Douglas Skyraider, one of the most long-serving aircraft of all time, as a torpedo bomber originally and used it in this role for the last time during the Korean War. On 4 May 1954 the Hawchon Dam was demolished by Skyraiders using aerial torpedoes when ordinary bombing failed. The dam was blown up to break up Communist grouping in preparation for the spring offensive.

It was the end of the torpedo bomber story.

Select Bibliography

Air Ministry, Official, *Despatches on the Operations of Coastal Command*, Royal Air Force, Air Ministry, London, 1950.

Bowyer, Chaz, *Eugene Esmonde*, VC, DSO, William Kimber, London, 1983.

Brown, Eric, *Wings of the Navy: Flying Allied Carrier Aircraft of World War II*, Jane's, London, 1980.

Davies, Richard Bell, *Sailor in the Air: the Memoirs of Vice Admiral Richard Bell Davies*, Davies, London, 1967.

Gibbs, R. P. M., *Not Peace but a Sword*, Cassell, London, 1943.

Grey, C. G., *Sea-Flyers*, Faber & Faber, London, 1942.

Halley, James J., *Famous Maritime Squadrons of the RAF*, Hylton Lacy, Windsor, 1972.

Harrison, W. A., *Swordfish Special*, Ian Allan, Shepperton, 1977.

Hurren, B. J., *The Swordfish Saga: Story of the Fairey Swordfish Torpedo Bomber and a History of Torpedo Plane Development in the Royal Navy*, Fairey Aviation, Hayes, 1946.

Hyde, H. Montgomery, *British Air Policy between the Wars*, Heinemann, London, 1976.

Jackson, Robert, *Strike from the Sea: a Survey of British Naval Air Operations 1909–69*, Barker, London, 1970.

Joubert de La Ferte, Philip, *Birds and Fishes; the Story of Coastal Command*, Hutchinson, London, 1960.

Judd, Donald, *Avenger from the Sky*, William Kimber, London, 1985.

Malizia, Nicola, *L'Aeronautica Militare Italiana*, Edizioni dell'Ateneo & Bizzarri, Roma, 1979.

Melhorn, C. M., *Two-Block Fox: The Rise of the Aircraft Carrier 1911–29*, Naval Institute Press, Annapolis, 1974.

Nesbit, Roy Conyers, *The Strike Wings: Special Anti-shipping Squadrons, 1942–1945*, William Kimber, London, 1984.

Nesbit, Roy Conyers, *Torpedo Airmen: Missions with Bristol Beauforts 1940–42*, William Kimber, London, 1983.

Peattie, Mark R., *Sunburst: The Rise of Japanese Naval Air Power, 1909–1941*, Naval Institute Press, Annapolis, 2001.

Popham, Hugh, *Into Wind; a History of British Naval Flying*, Hamish Hamilton, London, 1969.

Rawlings, John D. R., *Pictorial History of the Fleet Air Arm*, Ian Allan, Shepperton, 1973.

Rotherham, G. A. 'Hank', *It's Quite Safe Really*, Hangar Books, Belleville, 1985.

Schofield, B, *The Attack on Taranto*, Ian Allan, Shepperton, 1973.

Smith, Peter C., *Ship Strike: the History of Air-to-Sea Weapon Systems*, Airlife Pubishing Ltd, Shrewsbury, 1998.

Smith, Peter C., *The Sea Eagles: the Luftwaffe's Maritime Operations, 1939–1945*, Greenhill, London, 2001.

Smith, Peter C., *Midway: Dauntless Victory*, Pen & Sword, Barnsley, 2007.

Sturtivant, Ray, *Fleet Air Arm at War*, Ian Allan, Shepperton, 1982.

Sueter, Rear Admiral Murray F., *Airmen or Noahs*, Pitman, London, 1928.

Till, Geoffrey, *Air Power and the Royal Navy, 1914–1945: a Historical Survey*, Jane's, London, 1979.

Turnbull, A. D. and Lord, C. L., *History of United States Naval Aviation*, Yale University Press, Newhaven, 1949.

Vicary, Adrian, *Naval Wings: Royal Naval Carrier-Borne Aircraft since 1916*, Patrick Stephens Ltd, Bar Hill, Cambridge, 1984.